The British Press and Broadcasting since 1945
Colin Seymour–Ure

 KU-201-120

Third Party Politics since 1945
John Stevenson

British Science and Politics since 1945
Thomas Wilkie

British Public Opinion
Robert M. Worcester

Forthcoming

British Industry since 1945
Margaret Ackrill

The Conservative Party since 1945
John Barnes

The British Monarchy
Robert Blackburn

The Labour Party since 1945
Brian Brivati and Andrew Thomas

Electoral Change since 1945
Ivor Crewe and Pippa Norris

Religion in Britain
Grace Davie

Foreign Policy since 1945
Anne Deighton

British Social Policy since 1945
Howard Glennerster

Sport in Britain since 1945
Richard Holt and Tony Mason

Parliament since 1945
Philip Norton

The Trade Union Question in British Politics
Robert Taylor

The Civil Service since 1945
Kevin Theakston

British Foreign Policy since 1945
Geoffrey Warner

Terrorism since 1945
Paul Wilkinson

Making Contemporary Britain Series

General Editor: Anthony Seldon
Consultant Editor: Peter Hennessy

Published

Northern Ireland since 1968
Paul Arthur and Keith Jeffrey

The Prime Minister since 1945
James Barber

British General Elections since 1945
David Butler

The British Economy since 1945
Alec Cairncross

Britain and the Suez Crisis
David Carlton

The End of the British Empire
John Darwin

British Defence since 1945
Michael Dockrill

Britain and the Falklands War
Lawrence Freedman

Britain and European Integration since 1945
Stephen George

Consensus Politics from Attlee to Thatcher
Dennis Kavanagh and Peter Morris

The Politics of Immigration
Zig Layton–Henry

Women in Britain since 1945
Jane Lewis

Britain and the Korean War
Callum Macdonald

Culture in Britain since 1945
Arthur Marwick

Crime and Criminal Justice since 1945
Terence Morris

Third Party Politics since 1945

£11.99

WP 0820913 8

Third Party Politics since 1945

Liberals, Alliance and Liberal Democrats

John Stevenson

UNIVERSITY OF WOLVERHAMPTON
LIBRARY

Acc No.
820913

CONTROL

DATE
12. MAR. 1993

SITE
DY

CLASS
329
.941
STE

324.
2406
STE

BLACKWELL
Oxford UK & Cambridge USA

Copyright © John Stevenson, 1993

The right of John Stevenson to be identified as author of this work has been asserted in accordance with the Copyright, Designs and Patents Act 1988.

First published 1993

Blackwell Publishers
108 Cowley Road
Oxford OX4 1JF
UK

238 Main Street, Suite 501,
Cambridge, Massachusetts 02142
USA

All rights reserved. Except for the quotation of short passages for the purposes of criticism and review, no part of this publication may be reproduced, stored in a retrieval system, or transmitted, in any form or by any means, electronic, mechanical, photocopying, recording or otherwise, without the prior permission of the publisher.

Except in the United States of America, this book is sold subject to the condition that it shall not, by way of trade or otherwise, be lent, resold, hired out, or otherwise circulated without the publisher's prior consent in any form of binding or cover other than that in which it is published and without a similar condition including this condition being imposed on the subsequent purchaser.

British Library Cataloguing-in-Publication Data

A CIP catalogue record of this book is available from the British Library.

Library of Congress Cataloging-in-Publication Data
Stevenson, John, 1946–
    Third party politics since 1945 : Liberals, Alliance and Liberal Democrats / John Stevenson.
      p.   cm. — (Making contemporary Britain)
    Includes bibliographical references and index.
    ISBN 0–631–17126–6 (acid-free paper); 0–631–17127–4 (p.bk.)
    1. Great Britain–Politics and government–1945–   2. Center parties–Great Britain–History–20th century.   I. Title.
II. Series.
DA589.7.S74   1993
324.241′095—dc20   92–28891
                                          CIP

Typeset in 11 on 13pt Ehrhardt
by TecSet, Wallington, Surrey

Printed in Great Britain by T. J. Press (Padstow) Ltd., Padstow, Cornwall.

This book is printed on acid-free paper.

Contents

Tables

General Editor's Preface

The Institute of Contemporary British History's series *Making Contemporary Britain* is aimed directly at students and at others interested in learning more about topics in post-war British history. In the series, authors are less attempting to break new ground than presenting clear and balanced overviews of the state of knowledge on each of the topics.

The ICBH was founded in October 1986 with the objective of promoting the study of British history since 1945 at every level. To that end, it publishes books and a quarterly journal, *Contemporary Record*; it organizes seminars and conferences for school students, undergraduates, researchers and teachers of post-war history; and it runs a number of research programmes and other activities.

A central theme of the ICBH's work is that post-war history is too often neglected in British schools, institutes of higher education and beyond. The ICBH acknowledges the validity of the arguments against the study of recent history, notably the problems of bias, of overly subjective teaching and writing and the difficulties of perspective. But it believes that the values of studying post-war history outweigh the drawbacks, and that the health and future of a liberal democracy require that its citizens know more about the most recent past of their country than the limited knowledge possessed by British citizens, young and old, today. Indeed, the ICBH believes that the dangers of political indoctrination are higher where the young are *not* informed of the recent past.

The series contains two books to be published shortly, on the Conservative Party (by John Barnes) and on the Labour Party (by Brian Brivati). They are preceded by this volume, which is their necessary complement. Not only have both major parties' performance at elections been influenced by the third party, but the 'third force', comprising not just the Liberal Party but also in the 1980s the Social Democratic Party, is important in its own right to an understanding of post-war British history.

John Stevenson's book combines succinct narrative of the principal contours of the Liberal Party's post-war history with shrewd analysis. The first chapter charts the Liberal Party's fortunes from its replacement in the 1910s and 1920s by Labour as the second party in Britain's two-party system, until the Second World War.

The Liberal Party's bleakest period between 1945 and the late 1950s is the subject of the second chapter. These were the years when the great party of Gladstone, Asquith and Lloyd George all but disappeared. Six reasons are given for the party's survival. The final factor, Stevenson mentions, is that by the late 1950s the party was the only effective alternative to the two main parties: thus, when disillusion with Conservative and Labour parties manifested itself from the 1960s, it was the Liberals who were the main beneficiary.

The Liberal revival has traditionally been dated to the accession as leader of Jo Grimond in 1956, with the Torrington (1958) and Orpington (1962) by-elections, matched by dynamic gains in municipal contests in the early 1960s, proving high points in Liberal fortunes. The 1964 and 1966 general elections, however, showed that the promise of the early 1960s could not readily be turned into a significant number of seats in general elections. The 1970 general election proved even worse, with the 1966 total of twelve seats being cut to just six. In his third chapter, Stevenson also recounts the second Liberal 'bubble', in the early- to mid-1970s, which flowered into the Lib–Lab pact of 1977–78.

The fourth and fifth chapters analyse the time of the greatest potential for the Liberals, the 1980s, when in alliance with the

SDP, the Labour–Conservative duopoly of seats in Parliament appeared to be under serious threat. The 1992 General Election proved, however, the latest in a long series of disappointments. A masterly overview chapter concludes the book, drawing deep on the author's knowledge of both the party and the history of Britain during the entire century.

Anthony Seldon

Acknowledgements

This short book owes much to the work of other people. In particular, I would like to express my gratitude to Malcolm Baines who gave me free access to his work on the history of the Liberal Party before and after the Second World War and to Chris Cook whose *A Short History of the Liberal Party, 1900–1988* proved an invaluable guide. I would also like to thank Sue Sharman and Anne Borg who carried out most of the typing.

1 Introduction

In the decade or more following the Second World War Britain seemed to have established a stable two-party democracy. Reading British history selectively, it was possible to argue that a two-party system was 'natural' and that following a period in which the Liberal Party and the Conservative Party had been the main political rivals, Labour had risen between the wars to supplant the Liberals as the principal opposition party to the Conservatives. In the years after 1945, a dwindling Liberal Party looked on the road to extinction, faced with two other parties which completely dominated electoral representation in the House of Commons. The Liberal revival from the late 1950s, however, began a process which was to make third-party politics a significant factor. With a rise in Liberal success in the 1970s it became clear that the electoral situation was becoming more complex, a view reinforced by the growth of Nationalist parties in Wales and Scotland and the appearance at elections of significant bodies of candidates from the extreme left and the extreme right.

The formation of the Social Democratic Party (SDP) in 1981 and the creation of the Alliance with the Liberals transformed the outlook for third-party politics. For a short period it appeared that a major realignment was about to take place in British politics. As it turned out, this did not happen, but with almost a quarter of the popular vote in the two general elections of 1983 and 1987 the Alliance established itself as a significant third force in parliamentary elections and in local government, although denied a proportionate share of MPs. Shortly afterwards, the merger negotiations and quarrels between the new merged party and a 'continuing SDP' created such a serious hiatus that it almost appeared that the third party had destroyed itself, returning politics once again to a two-party system. However, within three years of its formation the Liberal Democrats had re-established a viable third-party position, retaining a solid basis in local government, a return to by-election successes and a rising position in the opinion polls. In the run-up to the 1992 General Election, the Liberal Democrats had shaken off the challenge of the rival fragment of the old Alliance, David Owen's 'continuing SDP', had seen the containment of the Green Party and was once again making a significant third-party challenge.

In retrospect a less selective reading of modern British political history reveals that it was not the emergence of a three-party contest in the 1980s which was exceptional, but the period of apparent two-party dominance after the Second World War. At least from 1906, when the newly-formed Labour Party captured 30 seats, until 1945 there was never a simple two-party system in the House of Commons. Until the end of the First World War it included not only Labour but also the Irish Nationalists. After 1918 the Conservatives, Labour and the Liberals competed in what became during the 1920s effectively a three-party system, further complicated by divisions for part of that time between the Liberal followers of Lloyd George and Asquith. Only after 1929 was the Liberal Party squeezed into a clear minority position. The 1930s saw further electoral complications with the creation in 1931 of a 'National' Government, drawing on Liberal, Labour as well as Conservative support. In the subsequent general election the back of the old Liberal Party was broken, dividing the Party once again into different camps, so that the Liberals fought the 1935 General Election in three fragments; 'Liberal Nationals' (supporters of the National Government), a group of independent Liberals and a small group of Lloyd George's supporters. In practice, the 1935 election had been essentially a two-horse race between Labour and the 'National', but now largely Conservative, Government. The 1945 election saw further development on the two-party system with the lion's share both of the popular vote and of seats being taken by the Labour and Conservative parties. Not only was the independent Liberal Party reduced to a rump of twelve seats, but other rival political formations such as Acland's progressive, anti-Tory Commonwealth Party, dismally failed to achieve a breakthrough as viable parties in the House of Commons. The decade after 1945 saw the two-party system consolidated. The Labour and Conservative parties took an increasingly large percentage of the popular vote, while there was some further rationalization of parties. The former Liberal supporters of the National Government of the 1930s, the Liberal Nationals were absorbed into the Conservative Party and Acland and many of his Commonwealth supporters into the Labour Party. Reduced to only six MPs in the early 1950s, the independent Liberal Party was faced with a massive Labour-Conservative duopoly which was to make the 1950s the high point of the two-party system.

During this period, the small remnant of the Liberal Party became a minority 'third' party. Indeed, after the coalescence of the other groups into the larger parties, the habitual adherence of the Ulster Unionists to the Conservatives and the inability of other parties to secure more than one or two seats in the Commons, the Liberal Party became, almost by default, *the* third party of British post-war politics. Although it was to come perilously close to extinction in the post-war decade, a series of revivals from the late 1950s provided a basis on which a third-party challenge could be sustained. The Liberals did so in a context from the 1970s in which a variety of other groups, such as the Nationalist parties, the National Front, various left-wing groups and, later, the environmentalists, also competed for political representation. None the less, in spite of serious competition from the Nationalist parties in Scotland and Wales in particular, the Liberals were able to sustain their position as the principal third-party challengers over the country as a whole. The Liberals, however, remained firmly in the position of a minority party offered only fleeting glimpses of power in the 1970s via the close results of elections and the possibility of striking a deal with another major party. The failure to find such an arrangement after the 1970 General Election and the short-lived Lib-Lab pact of 1977–8 left the Liberal Party still seeking a secure place for itself within a dominant two-party system.

With the formation of the Alliance between the Liberals and the newly-formed Social Democratic Party in 1981, a credible third-party challenge reappeared for the first time since before the Second World War. In spite of initial success in raising third-party support to new heights, the failure to achieve an electoral breakthrough in terms of seats, to eliminate Labour as the principal opposition party and tensions within the Alliance created an impass by the time of the 1987 election. The attempt to create a more effective merged party served in the short term to fragment former Alliance support, bring about a collapse in poll ratings and all but destroy the credibility achieved since 1981. Only slowly was the new merged party, the Social and Liberal Democrats, able to rebuild a viable position and begin another revival of third-party support in the run-up to the 1992 election.

2 The Road to Ruin: The Liberal Party, 1900–1945

By the time of the 1945 election, the Liberal Party appeared the mere empty shell of a once powerful governing party. The Party had summoned up what energies it had left and fielded 306 candidates, more than in 1935 at the last pre-war election, but still only half the number of its opponents, Labour and Conservative. When the votes were counted, the Party found it had elected just 12 MPs in a House of Commons of 640 members. Amidst Labour's euphoria at its first clear majority at Westminster, the Liberal candidates had gained just 9 per cent of the total vote and 76 (a quarter) had lost their deposits, more in fact than at any previous election in the century. The Party which only 40 years earlier had returned 400 MPs in a general election, presided over the introduction of the rudiments of a welfare state, enjoyed the talents of the likes of Asquith, Lloyd George and the young Winston Churchill and had ruled the country either alone or in coalition continuously between 1906 and 1922, seemed destined to fill a place only as a footnote in electoral history. What had gone wrong? What had happened?

The strange death of Liberal England

Historians have usually given one of four answers, or a combination of them, to the reasons for the decline of the Liberal Party in the first half of the twentieth century. First, and for long influential, was the idea that the Liberal Party was already dying in the years before 1914; that its ideology and moral foundations in nineteenth-century Liberalism and nonconformity were becoming outmoded and under increasing and obvious threat in the run-up to the Great War. Second, there is the argument that the rise of a more class-based society, signified by the rise of mass trade unionism from the end of the nineteenth century and the formation of the Labour Party, spelt the end of the old two-party duopoly of Conservatives and Liberals. An increasingly organized and politically-conscious working class would inexorably turn to its own political party for expression, depriving the Liberals of the mass support they had once enjoyed as the party of reform and opposition to privilege. Third, and in contrast, others have pointed to the still relatively positive signs for the Liberal Party in the years before 1914, its continuing electoral dominance and its adoption of a 'new Liberalism' or 'progressivism' with which it sought to consolidate working-class support and adapt itself to new requirements, giving the Party at least a fighting chance of retaining a powerful position. Here, the culprit for Liberal decline was the Great War, in Trevor Wilson's memorable phrase the 'rampant omnibus' which ran the Party down as it attempted to re-invigorate its ideology and programme in the early twentieth century. The Great War forced the abandonment of many long-cherished Liberal principles of free trade and non-interference in the economy, forced the introduction of censorship and conscription and precipitated a wholesale plunge into the more extensive provision of state welfare and housing. The war also produced a damaging, almost mortal, split between Asquith and Lloyd George, bitterly dividing the Party and, not least, a radical extension of the franchise in 1918 whose effects were harmful to its long-term survival. Fourth, however, it could be argued that even with all these negative features, the real period of effective decline lay in the inter-war years. That, as late as 1929, the Liberals remained a potential party of government with enough candidates, adequate funds and an effective and distinct programme, has suggested to many that the real period of Liberal decline lay in the years after 1918.

The debate on the decline of the Liberal Party and its replacement between the wars by the Labour Party as the principal opposition to the Conservatives is one of the most complex in modern historiography.[1] None the less, the years after 1918 were to represent the transition from a potential party of government to minority status. The 1918 General Election saw the Party split and its overall vote reduced from the pre-war elections of 1910. The combined vote was a mere 26.6 per cent compared with over 49 per cent in both 1910 elections. Although the followers of Lloyd George were members of a victorious coalition and gained 133 seats, they had done so in circumstances of the 'Coupon' as approved coalition candidates. There were many who saw that if ever Conservative support was to be withdrawn the Party might find it hard to sustain that level of MPs. Moreover, the Asquith faction of the Party had plunged to humiliating defeat, securing only 28 seats out of 253 candidates. With only 12 per cent of the overall vote, the non-coalition Liberals were in no position to go it alone.

With such success as they had earned, the Liberals in 1918 were also conscious that the election had been fought in new and unfamiliar circumstances. The 1918 Franchise Act had virtually trebled the electorate, giving the vote to those men who remained without the vote and to women over 30. The resulting election had been notable for a major Conservative advance and for forward movement on the part of Labour, who had secured the election of 63 MPs. Although short of a huge breakthrough, the Labour Party had put up 388 candidates compared with a mere 56 in 1910, signalling its entry onto the scene as a major contender for the votes of a now more-nearly democratic electrorate. Strengthened by the war-time expansion of trade unionism and especially the growing identification of the major mining and industrial centres with Labour, the Labour Party was establishing a bedrock of support upon which it would build between the wars. The Liberal Party, however, was in retreat, racked by division, with many of its constituency parties in complete disarray, and vulnerable to the breakup of the coalition which might bring the full weight of the Conservatives against them while forcing them to meet the challenge of a Labour Party confident in its new-found strength.

Thus, the immediate post-war period has been seen as the one in which the odds became stacked against the Liberal Party. This was not the same, however, as the suggestion that the process was irreversible or inevitable. The influential arguments that Liberalism was doomed by 1914 and that the rise of Labour was a certain consequence of class-based voting seriously underestimate the still considerable degree of regional variation in voting and the capacity the Liberals might still have had for revival. Nor does it seem that there was a simple correlation between the new voters and the rise of Labour. In many instances the new voters did not go over to the Labour Party; often it was the Conservatives who were the principal beneficiaries. Hence, while the 1918 election has been seen as a hinge-point between the sectarian and religious-based allegiances of pre-1914 and the class-based allegiances of the inter-war years, there remains considerable evidence that the complexity of alignments offered no simple message to politicians. What was certain was that the circumstances of 1918 were ones which had seriously weakened the Liberal Party and left it faced with two other parties neither of whom had any long-term interest in its survival. The larger part of the parliamentary Liberals clung to the raft of the coalition but in a position which could not be sustained indefinitely against growing Conservatice restiveness.

The party in the wilderness

The ending of the coalition with the Conservatives in 1922 visited the Liberal Party with the threats implicit in its position in 1918. Three elections in three years during 1922–4 saw the Liberal Party reduced to a dismal position behind both the Conservatives and Labour. In the 1922 election the Lloyd George Liberals and the followers of Asquith fought as separate entities. Of the 144 candidates as Lloyd George Liberals only 60 were returned compared with 133 four years earlier. Asquith's section of the Party improved on its position on 1918 but still only elected 62 MPs out of 333 candidates. The combined total of Liberal seats were less than that of Labour who returned 142 seats on approximately the same share of the vote. Some Liberal 'gains' were pyrrhic victories, Asquith's

Liberals taking ten seats from the Lloyd George group; more striking were the losses. The Party lost heavily in mining seats where it had been strongly represented in the years before 1914; large urban seats were being lost in places such as South Yorkshire, industrial Scotland and South Wales. Successes in rural England and Wales did little to compensate for the loosening grip of the Liberals in urban industrial England.

The scale of the 1922 defeat led to moves towards reconciliation at constituency level. Hesitancy on the part of the leaders was overcome when the Conservative Premier, Baldwin, called an election in 1923 on the issue of Protection. By raising the one issue which went to the heart of a common Liberal identity, Baldwin managed to unite the warring factions in a way which had been impossible earlier. Asquith and Lloyd George patched up their differences sufficiently for a united Liberal Campaign Committee to be set up and an agreement reached that all candidates were to stand, undifferentiated, as Liberals. A united campaign fund was established, although in the event Lloyd George retained considerable autonomy, including his own headquarters and sizeable personal fund. None the less, a united electoral challenge allowed the Liberals to achieve 159 MPs with 453 candidates.

Unfortunately for the Party this satisfying improvement was over-shadowed by Labour's performance with 191 MPs elected. Not only had the Labour Party overtaken the Liberals in parliamentary seats but it also formed its first Government with all the enhanced status and credibility that this brought with it. Even more serious for the Liberal Party than the formation of a short-lived minority Labour Government was that two elections in two years had come close to exhausting the Party's funds. When a further election was called for October 1924 the Party was seriously embarrassed. Lloyd George was prepared to advance only £50,000 from his own funds, virtually the only large resources available to the Party. No less important, however, was the unwillingness of local Liberals to fight another campaign. There were only 280 candidates in place when Parliament was dissolved compared with the 450 which senior Liberals believed necessary to fight an effective campaign. At constituency level many Liberals opted for local pacts with the Conservatives. As a result the Party fielded only 340 candidates in 1924 compared with 552 Conservatives and 512 for Labour.

If the portents for the Liberals were poor, the out-turn was way beyond their worst imaginings. Not assisted by a lack-lustre campaign in which the Party offered little that could not be found in the other manifestos, the Liberal Party went down to a defeat which reduced it from a realistic contender for office, as it had been in 1923, to a mere rump of a party. The Conservatives were returned to power with 412 seats, Labour was reduced but still held 151, while the Liberals won only 40 seats. With its reduced candidature, the Party had taken only 18 per cent of the votes cast, but concentration had done little for its ability to defend its seats. The average percentage of the vote taken by each Liberal candidate was just under 31 per cent, too low to defend adequately even those seats contested. Many candidates defending Liberal-held seats found themselves at the bottom of the poll and the casualties included much of the Party leadership, among them Asquith. The Conservatives made massive inroads into the Liberal vote in rural and middle-class areas, taking no less than 105 seats, while the erosion of the urban-industrial seats by Labour continued. Not a single county constituency in England returned a Liberal, while the Party held a mere six of the 139 constituencies in the largest cities.

The 1924 election saw the effective demise of the Liberal Party as a potential party of government in the inter-war years. When Asquith was elevated to the Lords in 1925, the Party increasingly came under the control of Lloyd George who took over its leadership in 1926. He began what was to become its dominating motif for the best part of the next half century, the search for a secure place as a third party, one from which it might be possible to hold the balance of power and bargain for a change in the electoral system. Accordingly, Lloyd George set about a dynamic drive to improve the Party's prospects. His followers displaced those of Asquith in the Party organization and disbursements from Lloyd George's funds permitted a series of policy initiatives. The most significant was the 'Yellow

Book', *Britain's Industrial Future*, published in February 1928. In this a distinguished group of politicians, businessmen and economists, including John Maynard Keynes, put forward far-reaching proposals for planning the economy. This was followed in March of the following year by a report, *We Can Conquer Unemployment*, which offered an emergency programme of road building and construction to relieve unemployment. Armed with some of the most ambitious proposals to deal with Britain's economic problems and with the Lloyd George fund paying for extensive literature and propaganda, the Party appeared to have picked itself up from the floor for the general election campaign of 1929. The optimistic mood was seen in the number of candidates fielded, 513, with which Lloyd George hoped to hold the balance of power. The outcome was a bitter disappointment: although the Party had polled over five milion votes and raised its share of the vote to almost 24 per cent, it captured only 59 seats. On the other hand, Labour had emerged for the first time in its history as the largest party in the Commons and formed the second Labour Government.

On the positive side it appeared that the Liberals had achieved the balance of power, but this did little to help Liberals as the economic blizzard of 1929–31 destroyed the Labour Government and brought about major rifts within Liberal ranks. Once again, as in 1923, a major effort was followed by disillusion and severe problems of finance and organization. Defections from the Party began almost immediately and Lloyd George refused to continue his personal financial assistance after the summer of 1930. The effects were soon felt in the loss of full-time officials and the failure to contest by-elections. Amidst recriminations, the Party began to experience renewed splits over its attitude towards the Labour Government. By November 1930 these rifts had come into the open with the resignation of the Chief Whip Sir Robert Hutchinson and Sir John Simon declaring openly in the press that he wished for an alliance with the Conservatives to bring down the Labour Government. At a time when Lloyd George was holding friendly discussions with the Labour Government, offering support in return for a promise of electoral reform, the Party appeared to be falling apart. When Parliament adjourned at the end of July 1931 the Party was in a miserable condition. Hutchinson's successor as Chief Whip, Sir Archibald Sinclair, had resigned in March unable to hold the factions of the Party together in the House of Commons; in late June Sir John Simon resigned the Liberal Whip with two other colleagues; then in July the Party was delivered another blow when Lloyd George became seriously ill.

But the imminent issue of Party divisions was overtaken by the financial crisis of the summer of 1931 which forced the resignation of the Labour Government and the formation of a National Government headed by the ex-Labour Premier, Ramsay MacDonald. One of the casualties of the turmoil was a Bill for electoral reform which had eventually received its third reading in the House of Commons on 2 June 1931 and had passed the Lords on 21 July. Brought in by the Labour Government with Liberal support, though both parties denied that it formed asny kind of 'deal' between them, a Bill to introduce the alternative vote, the division of two-member constituencies and the abolition of university seats and the business vote, as well as provisions for controlling election procedures, offered some prospect that the Liberals as a third force would be able to make a better showing even with a reduced candidature and share of the vote. The Bill was substantially amended by the Lords, in particular to extend the system of alternative voting to only a limited number of constituencies, mangling the main provision of the draft Bill. The amendments awaited reconsideration in the Commons when the Bill was overtaken by the parliamentary recess and by the upheaval of the summer. The Bill never progressed any further, leaving the Liberals no nearer the hope of a more secure electoral base in subsequent elections.

Instead, the Party took comfort from its position in the new National Government formed in August 1931. Liberals obtained two seats in the Cabinet; with Lloyd George still recovering, taken by Sir Herbert Samuel as Home Secretary and the Marquis of Reading as Foreign Secretary. The first taste of high office for almost ten years, however, was soon made uncomfortable by Conservative pressure for an election which the Liberals had hoped to avoid. The opposition of Lloyd George and Samuel to an early dissolution of Parliament proved ineffective and brought the Party face to face with its own divisions once again as Sir John Simon and his pro-Conservative followers supported the call for an election. The 1931 General Election called for 27 October has always been noted for its devastating effect on the representation of the Labour Party who, divided and discredited by the fall of the second Labour Government, were reduced to a mere 52 MPs. But the position of the Liberals was scarcely better; the Party faced in three directions. Samuel and Reading had not resigned from the National Government, alienating Lloyd George who withheld any money from his fund. The 'Samuelites' fought the election as virtual prisoners of the National Government coalition but adopting a non-Conservative, anti-Labour stance; the 'Simonites' adopted a position more favourable to the Conservatives while Lloyd George sponsored his own small group of followers. The Samuelites fielded 122 candidates, many of whom faced Conservative opponents, had few funds and had little faith in the outcome of the election; it was hardly surprising that only 35 secured election. The Simonites had an easier task, for while they only fielded 41 candidates they often contested stronger Liberal constituencies and frequently had Conservative support which allowed 35 of these Simonites or 'Liberal Nationals' to be elected. Lloyd George's family group made up another small faction of four Independent Liberals.

The various Liberal factions had gathered 13 more seats than in 1929, but in many cases it had been in an artificial position where there was no Conservative opposition. Moreover, in contrast to Labour which had suffered a massive loss of seatss but still polled an impressive 6,649,000 votes, the combined Liberal vote had fallen by three million to under two and a quarter million. The events which followed served only to compound the misery. The National Government's decision to introduce an Import Duties Bill in March 1932 put the Liberal free-traders on the rack and increasingly distanced them both from the Government and from the Simonite Liberal Nationals.

They in turn set up their own 'Liberal National Council' to co-ordinate relations with the Conservatives. The division between the two wings of the Party was brought to a head in the course of 1932 following the Ottawa Imperial Economic Conference and the agreement to bring in a limited degree of protection. Samuel left the National Government taking with him his followers, while the Simonites increased their links with the Conservatives. As the dust of these divisions began to clear, one thing became apparent; if the Liberals were to survive as an independent force they had to oppose the National Government. Samuel's original position was to leave the Government but to operate from the Government backbenches as a sympathetic, but critical supporter. By 1933, however, there was increasing pressure from the constituencies for a move into opposition, not only on issues of policy such as unemployment but also to preserve some credibility for the Party as an independent and distinct force.

Whither Liberalism?

The events of 1929–33 had come close to bringing about the Party's disintegration in which the failure of a series of initiatives only seemed to make the position worse. The great effort of 1929 had proved a grave disappointment in terms of the harvest of seats; the flirtation with the minority Labour Government had effectively divided the Party without obtaining electoral reform; Lloyd George's cessation of funding left the party virtually bankrupt; and the formation of the National Government had proved a dangerous trap in which the Party was forced into an election it did not want and was hardly in a position to fight. The divisions in the Party were now virtually unbridgeable. For the followers of Simon, the distaste of supporting the Labour Government was followed by support for the largely Conservative National Government and their acceptance of positions in it following the election of October 1931. Both Simon and Runcunian took seats in the Cabinet in early November 1931, already some way along a trajectory which led eventually to the Liberal Nationals' fusion with the Conservatives. In contrast, the followers of Samuel gradually disentangled themselves from the 'captivity' they had willingly accepted in the summer of 1931 and were forced once again to begin the attempt to rebuild and re-define the Liberal Party as a discrete force.

There was little with which to rebuild nor any clear direction in which the Party could go. The effects of the tergiversations and splits of the early 1930s further eroded an electoral base which was visibly crumbling. For the two major parties the electoral battle of the 1930s was about who was to harvest what was left of the Liberal vote. By-elections told a story of continued decline after 1932 where the party was able to find the resources and energy to field a candidate. Where they did, the results were almost wholly bleak. Sitting MPs, candidates, benefactors and supporters deserted what to many appeared a sinking ship. Attempts to carve out a distinct identity for the Party proved especially difficult. The conservative economic policies of the National Government occupied much of what was the middle ground of politics. When Liberal opposition was expressed, as over support for the League of Nations, opposition to cuts in unemployment pay and social reform, it found that ground already camped on by the Labour Party. Thoughts of turning again to the 'Welsh Wizard' to lead a revival were frustrated by Lloyd George's determination to follow his own maverick course. In January 1935 he launched his 'New Deal' campaign, aiming to unite all those who opposed the National Government and supported 'progressive' policies. The campaign was not specifically aimed at the revival of the Liberal Party, indeed there were features of it which threatened to alienate some of the more financially orthodox sections of the Party and anyone wedded to a faith in free trade. Lloyd George's campaign did little to assist the Samuelite Liberals as they prepared for a general election. As ever, the Party was short of funds and the constituencies were having real difficulties in finding candidates. Some doubted whether as many as a hundred could be found. In the event, the Party adopted 159 candidates, more than in 1931, but a huge fall on 1929. Whole tracts of the country were uncontested by Liberals independent of the National Government. The results were as bad as many feared. Only 21 Liberals were returned with just over 6 per cent of the total vote. Even taking into account the virtually independent Lloyd George Liberals, comprising members of his family, the total vote was only 1,422,000, a further heavy fall on the performance in 1931. Salt was rubbed into the wound by the election of 35 Liberal Nationals, sheltered from Conservative opposition by their continued support for the National Government so that no Liberal National was faced by a Conservative candidate. On the face of it, the wing of the Liberal Party that had allied with the Conservatives was already the effective third party in British politics. Their apparent strength, however, was illusory. As with the earlier Liberal-Conservative coalition under Lloyd George, Conservative support was tantamount to a life-support system to the Liberal Nationals – once withdrawn there was little hope of their survival.

In effect, the only really independent third force in British politics remained the small band of 21 Liberals and the semi-detached supporters of Lloyd George, but whether counted in terms of the share of the vote or of the number of seats, there was only evidence of fragile support. Moreover, that was still drifting heavily towards the Conservatives. Although Labour made significant gains in the 1935 election of over a hundred seats compared with the disaster of 1931, its most important result was to confirm the dominance of the Conservatives who alone returned 388 seats and with their allies, Liberal Nationals, National Labour and other minor 'National' candidates, obtained 435 seats. Labour had put on almost two million votes compared with 1931 and raised its share of the vote from 31 per cent to 38 per cent, virtually returning to the number and share of votes which it had obtained in 1929. Its failure to capture the same number of seats as then, however, was a consequence of the success of the Conservative Party in 1931 grabbing the lion's share of the five million Liberal votes cast in 1929 and holding on to them in 1935. The 'squeeze' of the two other parties on the Liberal vote was disproportionately favourable to the Conservatives. Not only did the Conservatives gain 55 per cent of the vote in 1931 when they faced a Labour opposition in disarray, and a divided Liberal Party, but they were only a point or two lower in 1935 when the Labour Party was enjoying a considerable degree of revival and fought the general election in a mood of genuine optimism.

The success of the Consrvatives in obtaining a higher share of the Liberal vote enabled them to score an important victory in 1935. Labour found itself unable to win the middle ground in a number of critical parts of the country, as the Liberal vote which had supported the National Government in 1931 continued to do so in 1935. Nor was this merely a matter of voting for the Liberal partners of the Conservatives, the Liberal Nationals, but was represented by an additional three million votes for the Conservatives in both 1931 and 1935 compared with their performance in 1929 and their highest share of the vote in the whole inter-war period.

For the Liberal Party itself, there seemed a genuine prospect that it would disappear altogether or be left only with those representatives who claimed the Liberal name under the umbrella of a nominal National Government, as Liberal Nationals. At least as worrying as the precipitate decline in the Party's vote and number of seats was that there was no solid basis for the Liberal Party in any part of the country. Even the Celtic fringe, once one of the bastions of Liberal support, was no longer secure. The General Election of 1935 was followed by a by-election in Ross and Cromarty, a Highland seat with a strong Liberal tradition; the result was a humiliation in which the Party took only 4 per cent of the vote. The Party, too, had lost many of its better candidates; Herbert Samuel lost his seat at Darwen and Isaac Foot at Bodmin. Behind this crumbling facade, constituency organization was in a perilous state – many Liberal Associations had not survived the 1920s and more were to collapse or become virtually inactive in the course of the thirties. There was open speculation both within and without the Party about whether it had a future. In November 1935 *The Times* noted; 'The great mass of the still formidable Liberal vote had departed from them; and they can win seats only where the Liberals are mesmerised by traditions affectionately disposed towards them on personal grounds, or discontented with candidates of poor quality on the other side.'

These doubts were shared by leading Liberals themselves. Five days after the 1935 election Ramsay Muir wrote to Herbert Samuel that many were talking of winding up the Party and that while he felt that this would abandon up to three million pro-Liberal voters many constituency Associations were bound to disband as a result of their debts. His proposal was for the formation of a new middle party as an umbrella to make statements of Liberal aims without necessarily using the Liberal label. If successful, the old National Liberal Federation could be wound up and a new party formed free from the tarnished legacy of the past. Others, such as Lord Lothian, also took a very realistic look at whether the Party should continue, writing a few days after Muir that, 'It may prove to be the best, perhaps the only course, for Liberals to join one or other of the two main parties and liberalise from within'.

In the event, Lothian was reluctant to see the party terminated, he, like others, arguing that a possible break up of the National Government or of the Labour Party might still give the Party a role. Hence he advocated keeping the Party alive and hoping for a change in electoral conditions, possibly also of a revival of the cause of electoral reform. Where Muir and Lothian saw little option but to soldier on waiting for something to turn up, the new leader of the Liberals in succession to Samuel, Sir Archibald Sinclair, took a more active line. Arguing that the Liberals had done better than they had any right to expect and that with one and a half million votes – even at a low ebb – the Party had something with which to bargain, he set about building bridges with Lloyd George to secure his personal prestige for the Party, a programme of reorganization and a search for a strategy which would appeal to the voters and allow the Party to bargain from a position of strength. Closer links with Lloyd George and his family group were relatively easy to establish, the results of 1935 assisting both sides to see little future in continued rivalry. The organizational sequel to 1935 was the appointment of the Liberal Reorganization Commission under Lord Meston to examine the whole structure of the Party. His report was presented and discussed at a party convention in June 1936. This resulted in the end of the National Liberal Federation, dating back to 1877, and the formation of the Liberal Party Organisation. The aim was to create a single policy-making body for the Party, though its effects were to leave authority divided between different bodies, the Assembly, the party council, the executive and the leader. On the other hand the Parliamentary Party and the Whips were given greater powers. Little, however, was done to assist the constituencies, whose problems of declining memberships and dwindling funds were as pressing as ever. None the less, the reorganization, even with the limitations of a 'top-down' initiative, had some effect in rekindling a sense of purpose and assisting communication between the Parliamentary Party and the constituencies.

More difficult was finding a distinct identity for the Party. Its central dilemma was that many of the policies it wished to pursue were either unrealistic in the climate of the thirties or had been adopted by other parties. On the key issue of the economy the radical solutions to unemployment offered in *Britain's Industrial Future* had been abandoned during 1929–31, but Baldwin and the Conservatives made the traditional Liberal policies of retrenchment and fiscal soundness very much their own. After 1931 the Liberals were left with issues such as free trade, the rights of India and constitutional reform. Although it might rally the Liberal faithful free trade seemed to offer little prospect of attracting votes in the general drift towards protectionism and economic autarky which characterized the decade. Baldwin's relatively liberal position on India left little room for the Liberal Party to make headway, while electoral reform meant little to the electorate. On social issues and disarmament, there was little to choose between Labour and the Liberals; moreover, the energetic efforts by the Labour research groups and special interest groups to firm up Labour policy and to publicize their findings were difficult for the Liberals to match. With greater resources for publicity and the active support on the ground in the constituencies and in the trade unions,

Labour was usually in a much better position to make the running and achieve the credit for formulating alternative policies.

The fortunes of the Party on the eve of the Second World War could be read two ways. There were signs of a modest revival in 1937. After 12 by-elections since 1935 in which no Liberal candidates were put forward, the Party polled respectably in two by-elections in the West Country in the summer of 1937. There was evidence of a surprising degree of enthusiasm at annual Assemblies, such as that at Buxton in 1937, and a 'cost of living' camapaign to petition Parliament early in 1938 had some success in collecting thousands of signatures. But there was also considerable evidence that the chronic weakness of the party, particularly at local level, had failed to be remedied. On the electoral evidence the mini-revival of mid-1937 was a misleading omen. 1938 was a bleak year for the Liberals with only two Liberal candidates standing in the 18 by-elections that year. In contrast to the optimism of the previous summer, the result of the two liberal interventions at Aylesbury and West Derbyshire in May were a bitter disappointment. In spite of good candidates and sufficient money, the Liberal vote had defected either to Labour or to the Conservatives. The results were sufficiently worrying to be discussed at a special luncheon at the National Liberal Club. The conclusions were that the anti-socialist vote had been alienated by talk of a 'United Front', while at the same time allowing Labour to recruit heavily from more sympathetic Liberal voters. The decay of local constituency organization was recognized as a factor too, 'immense difficulty' being noted in obtaining any local Liberals to conduct a canvass.

The last point was in many ways the most telling, for in spite of the reorganization following the Meston Report and a degree of optimism that some kind of 'floor' in Liberal fortunes had been reached, there seemed to be no let up in the chronic decay of the Party's grass roots which had been going on for most of the inter-war period. The percentage of candidates standing at municipal elections as Liberals was a barometer of the decay of local organization. Liberal candidates as a percentage of all candidates at municipal elections were as follows:

1922	18.0
1929	12.5
1931	9.8
1935	7.9
1938	5.6

That the Party was contesting only about one council seat in 20 by the eve of the Second World War was dramatic evidence of the decline in fighting spirit and activity at the local level. In almost every year the Party lost seats in municipal contests, so that the share of seats won had fallen over the decade from 14 per cent in 1931 to 10 per cent in 1935 and to just over 7 per cent by 1938. In many areas Liberals had ceased to be a presence at all; even where representation had still been relatively strong in 1930, such as the Midland boroughs, Liberal support had dwindled to insignificance by 1938 when they held only one seat in eight. In area after area, the temptation was for Liberals to join forces with Conservatives in an anti-socialist alliance. Often a gesture of weakness in finding candidates, money and workers at the local level, this policy played into the hands of the better organized and funded Conservatives. Usually it was only a short step from local pacts with the Conservatives to the disappearance of independent Liberal candidates from the scene altogether. Meanwhile, Liberals lost ground persistently to Labour in many of the Northern and Midland industrial areas, only a few isolated areas of strength remaining.

The outbreak of war in 1939 suspended normal political activity for the duration, the Whips of the three parties signing an agreement under which the general election (due in 1940 at the latest) would be held over and that the parties would agree to an electoral truce in by-elections while the war continued. Although there was some demur on the part of Liberals at ceasing political activity altogether, there was no evidence that another round of municipal contests, by-elections or a forth-coming general election would have seen anything other than a continuation of the same dismal story as in the preceding 20 years. The Second World War did little to interrupt that decline. Although the Liberals took their place in the war-time coalition, there was little hiding the fact that any future electoral contest would be one in which they would have only a walk-on part. The powerful mood of social optimism and reconstruction which swept the country in the war years was one which favoured the Labour Party not the Liberals. In the leftward shift among young intellectuals and writers of the late thirties, it was the Labour Party or even the Communist party which was the principal beneficiary. Compared with the galaxy of talent which clustered around groups such as the Fabian Research Bureau and the Left Book Club, the Liberal Party seemed increasingly out of date and redundant. It did have one of two stars. Sir William Beveridge, the author of the famous report on social insurance in 1942 which set out the basis of the welfare state, was a Liberal whose credentials went back to the Liberal heyday of the years before the Great War. So, too, was John Maynard Keynes, whose economic ideas were to do so much to influence post-war economic policy. But these were chiefs without in-dians. The thousands of young men and women who voted for the first time in 1945, the children of the Slump, looked to the Labour Party to build the 'New Jerusalem' not the Liberals. In spite of some optimism on the part of the Liberals the results were to be a bitter disappointment. The Party's prospects seemed no better than they had been before the war. In some ways they were worse – Labour appeared to have swept all before it, making inroads for the first time into middle-class constituencies and capturing seats it had failed to secure during the inter-war years. Labour's high tide seemed to leave little room for Liberal revival or even survival.

Note

1   For a succinct review of that debate see P. Adelman, 'The decline of the Liberal Party, 1910–1931' and D. Tanner, 'The rise of the Labour Party', *Modern History Review*, 1, No. 2 (1989), pp. 17–19. See also J. Turner, *British politics and the Great War: Coalition and conflict, 1915–1918*, (Yale, New Haven and London, 1992), pp. 390–436.

3 Extinction or Survival, 1945–1956

From almost every perspective, the late 1940s and early 1950s represented the nadir of the fortunes of the Liberal Party in the twentieth century and, with it, of any significant third-party role in British politics. The period was to see the Liberals squeezed to a miniscule share of the vote in general elections and reduced from 18 MPs before the 1945 election to a low point of six seats after the 1951 election, a position in which they were to remain during the two subsequent elections. The corollary was the peaking of the dominance of the Labour and Conservative parties to the point where it seemed they would finish off the Liberals completely. During this period, there was a very real prospect that the Liberal Party would cease to exist as an independent political force, either throwing in its lot with another party and giving up its separate identity or collapsing into a private political association and ceasing to contest elections.

Into the whirlwind

The General Election of 1945 swept away the last vestiges of the Liberal Party's pretensions to being a contender for government or even a realistic third force. The Party had hoped for 500 candidates in the general election, but in the event only 307 had been nominated by polling day, an insufficient number, even if elected, to form a government. The Party had entered the election with 18 MPs and emerged with 12. It had widely expected to benefit from a mood of public weariness with Churchill, a view not mistaken in itself, but it had completely failed to gauge the extent to which this mood would be almost entirely to the benefit of Labour. There were few crumbs of comfort. Almost all the Party leadership had gone down to defeat. The leader of the party, Sir Archibald Sinclair, was defeated in Caithness and Sutherland; the Chief Whip, Sir Percy Harris, lost at Bethnal Green. Sir William Beveridge, whose enormous prestige as author of the war-time Beveridge Report gave him an almost talismanic significance, went down to defeat at Berwick-on-Tweed. Most pathetic of all was the fate of the general mass of candidates, over four-fifths of whom were fighting their first election. In a veritable massacre of the innocents the great majority of them found themselves at the bottom of the poll. The Party's candidates had averaged only 18 per cent of the poll, a long trail of lost deposits left in the seats they had contested.

Geographically, the Party was now pushed increasingly into the rural backwaters. It had all but ceased to exist as an urban party: many of its remaining footholds in urban areas were among the casualties: Bethnal Green, Wolverhampton East, Birkenhead East and Middlesbrough West. The municipal elections of the following November told a similar story. Only 92 Liberals were successful compared with 384 Conservatives and 1,372 Labour candidates. The Party had only been able to field 360 candidates in total. Major cities were left with only one or two Liberal councillors, or none at all: London, two; Leeds, one; Birmingham, none.

There was some attempt to rebuild. An eight-man Committee on Party Reconstruction was appointed and its report, *Coats off for the Future*, was presented to the Liberal annual Assembly in 1946. Some attention was given to financial matters, a foundation fund being launched with a target of £125,000 over a five-year period. This was intended to replace the now defunct Lloyd George Fund and reliance on a small number of wealthy donors and self-financing candidates. By 1949 the Party was at least solvent and there were some optimistic claims that constituency organizations were beginning to recover. The real question was whether the Party had any point in going on at all if it could not break out from the parlous electoral situation it found itself in. One means of adding to the Party's strength – by reuniting with the Liberal Nationals – was quickly closed off. Talks between the two groups had been held during the war but had collapsed over the Liberal Nationals' desire to continue the National Government when the war ended. In May 1947 the renamed National Liberal Party reached an agreement with the Conservative Party establishing joint Conservative-Liberal Associations where both parties had an organization. In effect, the agreement merged the National Liberals with the Conservatives. The question now was whether the independent Liberals might follow the same path.

Pacts or merger

On the face of it there were strong superficial reasons why it might happen. Liberals already had a long tradition of pacts with the Conservatives at local level, where it had proved mutually beneficial. Amalgamation at local level into Conservative-dominated groups such as the 'Citizen's Party' in Bristol or the 'Progressives' in Sheffield had also occurred. The experience of other countries, such as New Zealand or Australia, had also been of small Liberal parliamentary groups joining anti-socialist fronts. Any ideas that the Liberals might form a deal with the Labour Party aroused little genuine support in the Party. Most important of all, the Labour Party in the full flush of enthusiasm after their 1945 triumph were not in a mood for pacts or alliances with the Liberals. Dalton was openly contemptuous and for many Labourites it was an often-to-be-repeated line of 'if you think you agree with us, join us'. Indeed, there was a steady trickle from the Liberals of those who felt they could make common cause with the Labour Party in its vigorous, post-war incarnation. Richard Acland, Liberal MP for Barnstaple since 1935, moved via his short-lived but influential Commonwealth Party, formed in 1942, into the ranks of the Labour Party, taking a Labour seat from 1947. Sir Ernest

Simon, one of the Liberal Party's leading progressive and a nationally recognized expert on housing and town planning, joined the Labour Party in 1946. For many of those that remained the tide of collectivism by the Labour Party seemed a threat to Liberal values and it was not difficult to construct a scenario after 1945 in which the anti-socialist forces should join together to defeat it. Of the options available to the Party; replacing the Conservatives, reuniting the 'Liberal family' or coalition with the Conservatives, only the last appeared at all realistic.

Soldiering on was a possibility, but many felt that some kind of pact with the Conservatives represented the only realistic hope of avoiding complete dissolution. The key issue of individual freedom could obtain some support from both Liberals and Conservatives. Peter Thorneycroft's pamphlet, *Design for Freedom* (1947) was signed by 50 Conservatives and 50 Liberals, but the leadership of both parties remained cool about the issue before the 1950 General Election. At local level, however, there was more support for Liberal-Conservative pacts in general elections. This was to prove vitally important in two towns, Huddersfield and Bolton, where two seats in each borough offered the opportunity for a local pact which gave the Liberals the prospect of retaining one of the seats. The situation in Huddersfield indicated the advantages such pacts offered. Before 1945 the seat had been represented by a Liberal National. In July 1947 the two bodies of Liberals merged locally creating a strong body on the council. In 1948 the town was divided into two constituencies, West and East, which Conservative Central Office believed could both be denied to Labour in straight fights. Hence, when the local Liberals took the initiative in calling for a pact with local Conservatives to share the seats and Central Office declined to intervene, the Liberals were able to retain one of their few footholds in urban Britain. Similar arrangements in Bolton also allowed the Liberal Party to retain an MP. Both Huddersfield and Bolton were peculiar in being medium-sized boroughs with two seats and a reasonable Liberal strength at local level. Moreover, the Liberals were fortunate that the division of responsibility between Conservative Central Office and the local Conservative Associations allowed such agreements to go ahead if they were acceptable at local level.

Consideration of reuniting with the Liberal Nationals or forming a national pact with the Conservatives diverted much energy in the late 1940s. When the General Election of 1950 was called, the Party remained in a weak position. It managed to field 475 candidates, a significant improvement on 1945, but the effort was to prove fruitless. The Party managed a small increase in its total vote, to 2,621,487 and, on a larger turnout, virtually the same share of the vote as in 1945, 9.1 per cent. But with a much larger number of candidates this was effectively a further defeat: 319 candidates lost their deposits and the number of MPs elected shrank from 12 to nine. Time to recover was not allowed, only twenty months later, in October 1951, the country went to the polls again. Low morale, inadequate funds and a shortage of candidates left the Party able to field only 109 candidates. Not surprisingly its share of the total vote fell to a new low, to 2.5 per cent, and the number of MPs was whittled down further to only six. This humiliating defeat, following on from that of 1950, represented a major setback to Liberal fortunes. The intervening gap between the 1950 and the 1951 elections had been too short to devise a national strategy so that in 1951 the smaller number of candidates did not represent a targetting of the more winnable constituencies. Seats with favourable results in 1950 were left uncontested. Money was desperately scarce. Already trailing behind the amount spent per candidate in 1945 and 1950, the much smaller number of candidates in 1951 had still left the Liberals able only to spend £488 per candidate, compared with £658 for Labour and £773 for the Conservatives.

The disasters of 1950 and 1951 reinforced throughts of some kind of pact with the Tories. The success of the Huddersfield pact was a healthy reminder of the advantages to a Party that had virtually no safe seats. Earlier opponents such as Archibald Sinclair were converted by the 1950 result into advocates for a pact on the basis of some promise of electoral reform. By October 1950 most of the leadership were in favour of some sort of short-term alliance with the Conservatives, involving regional arrangements over seats. Churchill seemed to be prepared to keep an open door to such proposals, while the Huddersfield example, and the absence of deep fissures on policy between Conservatives and Liberals offered some basis for advance. Informal discussions on an alliance had taken place from 1947, as we have seen, but really only gathered serious momentum in 1950. On 7 March 1950 Churchill proposed a Select Committee on electoral reform. Conservative Central Office was cool about the idea, believing the Liberal vote was so 'soft' and its organization so loose and weak that there was little chance of the Liberals being able to deliver their side of any deal on the basis of electoral reform. Intermittent discussions between Liberal and Conservative MPs took place in the summer and autumn of 1950, but though Central Office outwardly co-operated, it remained lukewarm. The very weakness of the Liberals meant that they were not perceived as a threat and, equally, that they would be unable to guarantee any worthwhile support. For the Conservatives, then, the obvious alternative was simply to wait and see without making any formal deals. It seemed more likely than not that the downward spiral of Liberal fortunes would eventually bring them most of the Liberal vote in time without any disruption to the Tory faithful. Indeed, when Violet Bonham-Carter held discussions with Rab Butler and this leaked out to the press, there was some hostility shown by Conservative backbenchers. None the less, Butler went so far as to suggest to Churchill a possible platform of agreement between the two parties, based on a pledge of electoral reform. However, when in September 1950 Churchill put to the 1922 Committee the proposal of preserving 20–40 seats for the Liberals he was greeted with silence. By early 1951 the negotiations were over; in spite of the urgency with which some Liberals, notably Violet Bonham-Carter, saw the issue, no agreement was forthcoming.

Following the 1951 election Churchill offered a place in his Government to the Liberal leader Clement Davies and a Conservative-Liberal coalition in the Commons. It was a tempting offer for a party which had just been comprehensively trounced in an election and looked close to extinction. Predictably, earlier pro-alliance Liberals such as Bonham-Carter were in support. Clement Davies saw Churchill three times in late October 1951 and consulted his colleagues before taking the decision to soldier on alone. To many it seemed a genuine offer from a Government which already had a working majority and, if any rationale were needed, fitted in with Churchill's desire to form a broadly-based administration. Davies' refusal of the offer looked like a brave gesture from a drowning man. Liberal prospects were so bleak it was thought to be only a matter of time before the Party accepted the inevitable. As a result, subsequent Liberal approaches to the Conservatives were treated with very little seriousness. Central Office remained opposed in the face of a Liberal electoral performance in 1951 which any professional political analyst would have found virtually hopeless. Only one Liberal, Jo Grimond, had actually been elected in a three-cornered contest. Churchill's perhaps sentimental attachment to his old party and still lingering hopes of an alliance, helped to persuade the Conservatives not to oppose Clement Davies, the Liberal leader. On the evidence, three more Liberal seats would have been lost had Conservatives put up candidates against them. Not could the Liberal Party be said to be knocking on the door of a significant body of seats. Most defeats in 1951 had been by large margins; the Liberals had come second in only five seats, in only two of which could they conceivably have a chance in straight fights. To hard-headed realists in Conservative Central Office there was little that the Liberals had to offer. In contrast, the Conservatives saw themselves as resuming the process begun in the 1920s of gathering in the Liberal vote to the Tory fold. Time seemed to be on their side. As a result, a further approach from Lord Moynihan, Chairman of the Liberal Party Executive, for a limited number of constituency pacts was greeted with disdain by the Conservatives.

The failure of attempts at a Conservative-Liberal pact or alliance and Davies' refusal to accept Churchill's offer were of great significance. Had they come to fruition, there was every prospect that the Liberal Party would have gone the same way as the Liberal Nationals and disappeared from the scene as an independent political force. The past record of such pacts had usually meant eventual absorption into the larger partner and a blurring of identities in favour of the bigger and more numerous party. In part the talks had failed from a mismatch of espectations. The Conservatives looked to assimilation, as they had already secured with the Liberal Nationals, not a pact to the benefit of two independent and sovereign bodies. On the Tory side, therefore, there was no intention of ensuring the survival of the Liberal Party by some form of electoral reform or a number of constituency-level pacts which allowed the Liberals to remain as a significant political force. In addition, the Conservatives feared causing dissent in their own ranks either through electoral reform or through the allocation of a group of seats to the Liberals. A further ingredient was the evidence from the new science of opinion polling which suggested that the idea of a large and disciplined Liberal vote ready to be delivered as a bound captive to another party was something of a myth. From the Liberal point of view, the requirement was survival: however desperate their position they required electoral reform or a clear run in a number of constituencies to guarantee their independence. These were conditions the Conservatives would not meet; the Liberals appeared to be dying and there seemed no point in the Conservatives preserving them.

A Liberal identity

Paradoxically, then, it was the very weakness of the Liberal Party in the early 1950s that was one of the major factors in its survival. Neither Labour nor the Conservatives felt it worthwhile to make a deal to preserve a Party which seemed about to fade away. Weakness, too, allowed the Party to withstand the blows which rained upon it in the early fifties. The Party was forced to depend increasingly on the enthusiasm and resources of individuals and groups. A somewhat inchoate and disorganized sturcture had two advantages. First, it made it difficult to lead the Party into a Liberal-Conservative alliance agreed at national level and paralysed attempts to give it that decisive leadership which might have tempted the Party leadership to mount such an attempt. Second, the Party's dispersed structure meant that it did not know when it was beaten. Even as the Party nationally was going into what seemed like terminal decline, many Liberals could continue to think purely in local terms, fighting their particular patch almost irrespective of the national scene. Survival was in part to be at the price of an even more disparate Party whose real existence lay with its local groups and activists.

Whatever the long-term advantages this structure gave for survival, it could lead to desperately negative effects in particular loacalities. One of the most marginal seats in 1951 was Labour-held Bristol North-East, which as the old Bristol North was held by a coalition Liberal, then Liberal National, Mr R H Bernays from 1922 to 1945. After 1931 there was occasional intervention from an independent Liberal, the last being in 1950. Both Conservatives and Labour sought to bid actively for the Liberal vote in 1951 when the local Liberal Association was unable to put up a candidate. The Conservative put himself forward as a 'Conservative and National Liberal' candidate, while a large portion of the Labour election address was given up to an appeal to Liberals. For the Conservatives it was particularly important to win over a part of the independent Liberals if they were to secure a majority. At his adoption meeting the Conservative candidate predicted that if Mr Churchill were returned, no Liberal would regret it, while the Labour address included a long quotation from Attlee on the similarity between the Liberal and Labour Parties: 'All these things that the Liberals have worked for we have carried out'. The local Liberal Association found itself in a contradictory position. It condemned the Conservative's use of the 'National Liberal' description and even refused to send him the questionnaire which Liberal headquarters had designed to test non-Liberal candidates' views on Liberal issues in constituencies where no Liberal was standing. If a candidate gave satisfactory replies, the local Association might urge Liberals to support them. Later, however, the decision was revoked and both candidates received the questionnaire. This was of little help, as both Labour and

Conservatives had a 'standard' set of answers for use all over the country. In the event, the Bristol North-East Liberal Association decided not to give its followers a lead on how to vote. Three days before the poll, however, the Secretary of the Liberal Association came out in favour of Labour and spoke at an eve-of-poll meeting. This was met by a letter from several 'Liberals' urging support for the Conservatives, followed by the retort from the Secretary that these were not 'real' Liberals but 'National Liberals'. In the event, the Conservative victory in overturning a Labour majority of 4,000 was secured on the basis of winning over approximately two-thirds of the Liberal vote in 1950.[1]

Such confusions and problems of identity were hardly unexpected and the Parliamentary Party was scarcely in a position to give a strong lead. Clement Davies noted in 1950 that 'there is no Party but a number of individuals who, because of their adherence to the Party, come together only to express completely divergent views'. The Party represented a kaleidoscope of positions, bound together by sentiment and a generalized sense of what Liberalism stood for. Often split down the middle on particular questions, the Party could still attempt to push particular 'Liberal' issues, such as constitutional reform in the shape of reform of the Lords and electoral reform, regional issues and internationalism. There was also a growing pressure group within the Party for the cause of civil liberties. The besetting difficulty for the Party remained that of finding some kind of distinctive identity while the legacy of the Liberal splits between the wars was still being felt. This perception was recorded in one of the early war-time opinion polls in March 1942 which discovered that 87 per cent of those interviewed in sample areas had no idea of Liberal policy. This lack of a clear identity was carried through into the post-war elections. On the face of it the Party could claim to have stood in 1945 on a clear manifesto: they had been in favour of limited nationalization of the key public utilities, the railways and the mines, but stopped short of the wholesale nationalization programme of the Labour Party which, they argued, would merely perpetuate monopoly under state control. The Conservative claims to represent the small men were portrayed as bogus, in that they were the Party who represented 'big business' and existing monopolies. A healthy dose of free trade would be a better solution than private monopoly control on the one hand and public ownership on the other. With 'clean hands' and 'no axe to grind' the Liberal Party proclaimed itself the only true Party of freedom. On welfare issues, the Party also pledged itself to the abolition of poverty and want, arguing that the coalition government's espousal of the Beveridge Report would not succeed in abolishing poverty with the scales adopted for family allowances and old age pensions.

None the less, a difficulty for the Liberals was that the events of 1945–51 had established a broadly-based consensus on a degree of nationalization, which still left a mixed economy and a reasonably comprehensive welfare state. Dubbed ironically 'Butskellism' from the similarity of the positions of the Labour Chancellor Hugh Gaitskell and his successor after 1951, Rab Butler, it seemed to leave little distinct ground on which the Liberal Party could stand. More pertinent, the overwhelming impression Liberals seemed to give was of being anti- socialist and anti-collectivist. As the first post-war general election study noted of the issues in the 1945 election: 'The Liberals' care for freedom thus gave them ultimately more in common with the Conservatives than with the Labour Party'.[2] It was a perception widely reinforced after 1945 when both Conservatives and Liberals attacked the development of a socialist state. The difficulty was that the Conservatives appeared to be making the running on this issue, compromising whatever support the Liberals might obtain from it, while at the same time losing the pro-interventionist vote.

In spite of this difficulty, the Party continued to regard a group of issues as its own. The questionnaire sent out in 1951 asked questions about rival candidates' views on electoral reform, monopolies, personal freedom, the African protec- torates, trade barriers, devolution and equal pay. This was partly in response to a move by Clement Davies in April 1950 to consult Liberal MPs, Peers and the Party Committee in order to define a distinctive Liberal position. Free trade remained a problematic issue. After several years of a highly controlled economy, there were still those who saw free trade as a defining tenet of Liberalism. On the other hand, a Party increasingly confined to rural areas which depended on agricultural price-support for their prosperity could no longer glibly preach the abandonment of protection and subsidies. This created some tensions in the Party. In 1950 the Party accepted protection in agriculture but retained a commitment to reduction in tariffs. Three years later, however, the tables were turned at the Liberal Assembly when it voted for the gradual abandonment of guaranteed markets and fixed agricultural prices. Several prominent Liberals disagreed strongly, refusing to commit themselves to a policy which was bound to lose the agricultural vote. The 1955 manifesto, *Crisis Unresolved*, managed to look both ways, attacking subsidies as short-sighted, but aiming not to remove them until protective measures for agriculture were abandoned generally.

The Party also began to carve out a distinctive position for itself as an early voice against large-scale corporatism and private monopolies. This strand of the old radical inheritance was accompanied by increasing interest in co-ownership. A Liberal committee on monopolies in 1945 had devised a scheme which included co-ownership for all concerns with more than 50 employees or £50,000 in capital value. The 1948 Assembly subsequently adopted the principle of compulsory co-ownership. Although the element of compulsion was subsequently played down, it remained part of the Party's policy. On the welfare state, the Party continued to live off the capital of Beveridge though adding a commitment to equal pay for equal work for women. In the structure of government, the thrust of the policy was towards decentralization, devolution and a reform of the government machinery. Both the 1950 and 1955 manifestos contained paragraphs advocating proportional representation. In international affairs, the Party had inherited much of the pre-war idealism which had been invested in the League of Nations and translated it into support for the United Nations, so that at local level many activists were associated with groups such as the United Nations Association. Anti-communism and anti-imperialism also remained important issues, with consider-able concern for the plight of individuals, such as Seretse Karma, caught up in the prevailing legacy of racial bigotry and colonial attitudes.

The difficulty was that this was not really distinct enough. Only on free trade and proportional representation were the Liberals very far outside the Butskellite consensus. On many of the issues, the Liberals were easily outgunned by the Conservat-ives: freeing up the economy, a market economy, removal of tariffs and sound money. Certainly, some younger Liberals, such as Jo Grimond, felt that the Party had been too ready to embrace the post-war consensus and failed to carve out a distinct enough niche for itself in the public eye. This was probably asking too much for a Party with only six MPs after 1951 and with an increasing problem of obtaining any kind of hearing amidst the din of the two major parties. Only in the relatively august reviews of the Party election manifestos in the quality press prior to the elections did the Liberal Party's ideas get any significant airing. Public perception lagged a long way behind.

Organizationally the Party after 1945 had two almost parado-xical changes to accept. It had to come to terms with its shrunken status while at the same time adapting from a structure dominated by a few wealthy individuals to a mass membership. These features pulled in opposite directions; a Party which was dwindling in support found itself unable to field a convincing body of general election candidates without the patronage of the well-to-do. In 1950 sufficient candidates to form a government were only funded by the generosity of a few such Liberals. Of the Party's 475 candidates who fought in February 1950, only 250 had been 'in place' on Christmas Day, 1949. This was a sorry out-turn for the high hopes of a 'broad front' strategy proposed in the 1948 Liberal Assembly when the Party had established a fighting fund and candidates seemed to be coming forward. Candidates were solicited from the Oxbridge Liberal Clubs and drafted into the constituencies with a standard election address and a deposit which 319 did not save. The 1950 result prompted a change of strategy now that the broad front was discredited. The 'narrow front' in 1951 and, later, in 1955 was a response, but it was a strategy that was not well-handled in 1951, with some of the best seats of 1950 left uncontested. The Party's new General Director, HFP Harris, began work in March 1953 on a more systematic basis, aiming to 'target' up to twenty seats. The intention was to repudiate any seats fought without the approval of headquarters. This in itself caused some dissension, the cherished right of Liberal Associations to decide for themselves was threatened and there remained a problem of finding sufficient suitable candidates and adequate finance. The financial problem was particularly pressing. The Party's attempts to widen its financial basis had not reall worked. Liberal finances between 1945 and the mid-1950s remained heavily dependent on gifts, on the sale of *Liberal News* and on regional rallies. As the Party fell in numbers, reaching its lowest point about 1953, gifts from rich donors and the Assembly appeal became more important not less. By 1954 a quarter of the Party's income came from the Assembly appeal. Without the institutional backing of the unions for the Labour Party and of business for the Conservatives, the Party was forced to limp along in a weak financial condition – effectively living from hand-to-mouth.

The Party, too, inherited a weak constituency organization. Prior to 1945 it had often been the case that local elections were fought at fairly low intensity. Turnouts were small; only one LCC election between 1919 and 1946 had seen a poll of more than 40 per cent (43.4 per cent in 1937) and even Labour's great triumph in 1934 in taking control of the LCC had been won on only a 33.5 per cent turnout. There was a strong tradition, echoed both by middle-class Conservatives and Liberals, that canvassing in local and even national elections was slightly disreputable. Among Liberals, the idea that the 'right' policies were sufficient to attract the voters was deeply held. This rather high-minded view of the political process was increasingly abandoned by other parties after 1945, especially as the Conservatives and Labour began to square up to each other following the 1945 election. Liberal constituency organization often remained stuck in its traditional mode, relying on the personal vote for the local Liberal candidates. Sir Archibald Sinclair's defeat in Caithness and Sutherland came as a considerable shock and evidence that the old style of politics was no longer sufficient, even in remote rural areas where a strong sense of sturdy independence and personal loyalty had hitherto been sufficient. Under pressure even in the periphery of Britain, Liberal organization was unable to compete with the increasing professionalism of the larger parties in the mainstream of constituencies. The Party's organizational structure had failed to adapt to what was to become the dominant feature of its appeal in the middle and late 1950s as a place for disillusioned protest votes rather than traditional Liberal voters. Organization was extremely sketchy, made up of individuals and independent groups, to whom strong central direction was anathema. Areas of Liberal strength were as much characterized by networks of personal ties and political culture as by effective organization.

The seeds of revival

These features were to condition the performance of the Party in the aftermath of 1951. The Party failed repeatedly in by-elections to reverse its dismal performance in the general election. Moreover, the local base of the Party could not have been weaker. Several decades of decay at local level left the Party acting as a minor voice in municipal politics, contesting only a fraction of seats and winning only a tiny proportion of the total each year. Only 72 Liberal councillors were elected in 1950 out of a total of 3,324. By 1952 it had fallen to 53 out of 3,397 and by 1955, the year of the general election, 56 out of 3,644. This was a mere 1.5 per cent of the total and compared with more than around 1,500 councillors elected by each of the other parties. This was the background against which the Liberals fought the 1955 General Election. The Party fielded 110 candidates, maintaining the 'narrow front' approach of 1951. The result was little different; the total Liberal vote was under three-quarters of a million, representing 2.7 per cent of the total votes cast. Sixty candidates lost their deposits, but at least the total of MPs remained at its pre-election number of six.

The Party failed to gain any seats, but had not lost any; its share of the vote per candidate rose very slightly from 14.7 per cent to 15.1 per cent.

The campaign had revealed all the old problems. Even with a narrow front strategy which the Party had had more time to prepare, there were serious weaknesses. The financial position of the Liberal candidates was, even with limited numbers, worse than their rivals, the amount spent per candidate falling from £488 in 1951 to only £423 in 1955, well short of the other parties. At an organizational level in the constituencies, the Party was well behind its rivals with only 32 full-time agents. The series of election studies of the Bristol North-East constituency revealed a not untypical situation. Fought in 1950 when the Liberals gained over 4,800 votes, left uncontested in 1951, the Liberals decided to fight Bristol North-East in 1955 as part of their narrow front. The Liberal decision to fight was based on a relatively favourable record of municipal activity, having fought two of the four wards in the constituency in municipal contests since the war. In fact one ward had been contested once, the other twice. This 'good' record compared favourably with the rest of Bristol but was a not untypical picture of the feebleness of urban Liberalism by 1955. The seat was also highly marginal, one where Liberal intervention could have most impact. Although the decision to fight the seat was taken as early as July 1954, the Liberals had done little preparatory work apart from what was somewhat optimistically termed 'preliminary canvassing' – cards were handed out to electors who were to sign and return them if they were Liberals. Even this was only carried out in one part of the constituency. The account of the Liberal organization told a not unfamiliar story:

The divisional organization was still extremely weak in May, 1955, and some supporters were old ladies, unable to canvass. There was no full-time agent or secretary, no ward organization and no Young Liberal Branch. Moreover, there was no prospective candidate until April, 1955, when Mr George Stevenson, a Bath City councillor, was chosen. Mr Stevenson, a chiropodist, was able to 'make' some free time for nursing the constituency, but still had to keep his business going. When the election was

announced, the Liberals had no full-time agent. Neither did they
have a full-time agent *during* the election. They calculated that it
would cost £12 a week for several weeks, a sum they could not
afford. The secretary of the Bristol Liberal Council. . . acted as
agent during the election, but was available only at the evenings
and at weekends. His only leave of absence from employment
was on election day itself. . . When the campaign began, the
Liberals *stopped canvassing*! Even with help from the rest of the
city. . . they had so few workers that they all had to be employed
in sending out the election address.

This was the local reality behind the national performance of the
Liberal Party in the 1955 election and in a constituency the
Party had chosen to fight as one of their better prospects for a
respectable showing. In the event, the Liberals in Bristol
North-East managed to obtain over 4,000 votes, a 'remarkable'
achievement, according to the later study, in view of the
'shoe-string' organization run by the Liberals. The Liberal
votes, they concluded, 'were gained by a third party living on its
traditions, with virtually no organization whatsoever'.[3]

The 1955 election marked a significant point in the Liberal
Party's history and, in retrospect, for the future of third-party
politics in Britain. The 1955 election was the first election since
1929 in which the Party had made any improvement on its
previous performance. It had also halted the decline in its
number of parliamentary seats, although at a precariously low
level. The Party still had a number of MPs which allowed it still
to feel that it represented a significant presence in the House of
Commons. It is a matter of speculation, but six MPs allowed the
Party a degree of credibility which it would have been impossible to retain had it been reduced to only two or three.
Above all, the Party had survived. In spite of having only a
handful of MPs compared with its 20 before the Second World
War, it had managed to retain a presence. Whatever its
organizational and financial weaknesses, its narrow electoral
base in the rural backwaters of Britain and its clearly minor-
party status, there was still something on which the Party might
be rebuilt.

How had it survived? There were a number of reasons. First, the Party couls still depend in the 1950s on a traditional Liberal vote, now much shrunken, but still providing some kind of basis for survival. All the constituencies that returned MPs after 1945 had formed part of the Liberal heartland before 1914: the Celtic fringe, rural areas and old centres of Liberal radicalism and nonconformity, such as West Yorkshire. The same was true of its municipal base where some vestigial elements of organization remained in Liberal Clubs, Associations and a small number of councillors. Second, the pacts in parliamentary seats such as Bolton and Huddersfield were of quite disproportionate significance as a lifeline to the Party during its decline into the 1950s, helping to keep its parliamentary strength at a level which allowed it to retain some credibility as a national force. The peculiar situation of the boroughs concerned and the Conservative desire to maximize Labour losses following their drubbing in 1945 assisted Liberals at a time when their fortunes were at their lowest ebb. Third, the Party's structure as a loose grouping of largely middle-class individuals, tied together by sentiment, friendship and voluntary commitment, was one well-adapted to survival and to resisting take-over. Like some declining Nonconformist sect – a parallel which was not without significance for a Party which still often depended for its personnel and recruits upon the 'Nonconformist conscience' – the Party retained something of the character of an 'organized moral force' which was only partly concerned with the business of winning elections. Where a more professional organization might well have given up the struggle, the Liberals tended to persist, flying the flag for values and principles which still had some meaning for its participants. Fourth, the memory of the Party's distinguished history was still only just over the horizon in the late 1940s and early fifties. The Party could still trade upon its traditions, even if now somewhat faded, to recruit a cadre of new activists and to maintain clubs at the universities, north and south of the Border, which still provided a body of well-qualified, articulate candidates and spokespersons for the Party. While the major parties might have been winning the majority of the popular vote and gaining the lion's share of those actively involved in politics, the Liberal Party retained just sufficient numbers of talented people to sustain an element of continuity and, ultimately, to provide it with fresh leaders and candidates. Fifth, as we have seen, the very weakness of the Party by the late 1940s and early 1950s meant that its absorption by one of the other parties did not seem a worthwhile effort for the disruption and discomfiture it might cause. The contempt with which the prospect of a deal was viewed either by Labour or by many Conservatives was itself conducive to the survival of a separate Liberal Party. To the professional analysts at Central Office, in particular, it seemed pointless to waste energies in taking over a party which seemed doomed to dwindle into insignificance.

Finally, the Liberal Party benefitted in a curious way from a political system which in other ways disadvantaged it. While suffering from the effects of the 'first-past-the-post system' in not getting a share of seats proportionate to its share of the popular vote, other minority parties found it even more difficult to obtain a significant foothold in the House of Commons. After the effective absorption of the Liberal Nationals into the Conservatives, the Liberals were left as the only third party which commanded a handful or more of MPs in the house. With the exception of the Ulster Unionists who usually took the Conservatives Whip, there was, in fact, no other grouping to compete with the Liberals for the third-party position. Communists and fascists had failed before the war to achieve significant parliamentary representation. The Independent Labour Party had three successful candidates in 1945 but in 1946 they joined the Labour Party. Richard Acland's Commonwealth Party similarly failed in 1945, shattering his hopes for a new progressive grouping. Weslsh and Scottish Nationalist candidates were also largely unsuccessful in the critical period between 1945 and the Liberal revival in the late 1950s, as were to be the neo-fascists of Mosley's Union movement. For good or ill, the Liberals were to retain sole effective third-party status long enough for them to benefit from the effects of a revival of support for an alternative to the two main parties.

Notes

1   R.S. Milne and H.C. Mackenzie, *Straight fight: a study of voting behaviour in the constituency of Bristol North-East at the General Election of 1951*, (The Howard Society, London, 1954), pp. 75–7.
2   R.B. McCallum and A. Reedman, *The British General Election of 1945*, (Oxford University Press, Oxford, 1947), p. 62.
3   R.S. Milne and H.C. Mackenzie, *Marginal Seat, 1955: a study of voting behaviour in the constituency of Bristol North-East at the General Election of 1955*, (The Howard Society, London, 1958), pp. 18–20.

4 The Liberal Revivals, 1956–1981

The period from the late 1950s to the late 1970s was notable for the Liberal revival which carried the Party from the brink of extinction to a reasonably secure presence in Parliament, saw a revival in voting strength to a peak of over six million, a growing, substantial presence in local government and two opportunities, one taken up, to participate in government. The Liberal revival was a complex process which contained within it a series of surges of support, with intervening setbacks, amidst a long-term loosening of the dominance achieved by Labour and the Conservatives in the decade after the Second World War. Moreover, the Liberals were not the sole beneficiaries of these developments. By the 1970s, a proliferation of other political groupings, most notably the Scottish and Welsh Nationalists, were beginning to represent a significant force. It was the Liberals, however, who led the field and their revival which marked the major theme in third-party politics.

In retrospect, the general elections of 1951 and 1955 were a significant watershed in the larger context of British electoral sociology since 1918 and also of third-party politics. They marked the high-point of the two-party hegemony measured in share of the popular vote and the number of seats. In both elections, Labour and the Conservatives between them took over 96 per cent of the vote and all but a handful of the available seats in Parliament. Neither before nor since have two parties enjoyed such a complete dominance in British parliamentary elections. With six seats in 1951 and 1955, the Liberals remained the only representatives of a possible third force in

British politics, albeit at the nadir of their fortunes. In fact, the 1955 election was to mark a turning point for the Liberal Party and for third-party politics in Britain. After that point the Liberal revival began.

The seeds of revival

The conventional picture of the Liberal revival usually begins in 1956 with the accession of a new leader, Jo Grimond, who more than anyone else was identified with the revival of Liberal fortunes. Whatever his other merits, the incumbent leader, Clement Davies, now aged 72, was no longer a force to revitalize the Party. Grimond, aged only 43, was both dynamic and enthusiastic for the challenge of raising its flagging morale and status. Significantly, he had built up his seat in Orkney and Shetland into one of the few secure bases the Party still possessed. There was, however, some evidence of a pro-Liberal movement in the electorate even before Grimond took over. In December 1954 a Liberal who had not previously contested the seat in 1951 secured 36 per cent of the poll at a by-election in Inverness. There was also evidence from the 1955 General Election that the Liberals were beginning to attract a 'floating' or protest vote, those wavering in support or those wishing to protest against the existing government without switching their allegiance to the other major party. Thus in Bristol North-East two-thirds of a sample of Liberal voters in 1955 had not voted Liberal before.[1] This was reinforced by further by-election successes before Grimond took over the leadership. At the Torquay by-election in December 1955, the Party took almost a quarter of the vote, not sufficient to win the seat, but a considerable improvement on its performance in the general election the previous May. In February 1956, Frank Owen managed to obtain 36 per cent of the vote at Hereford, pushing Labour into third place.

These straws in the wind antedated the resignation of Clement Davies at the Folkestone Assembly on 29 September 1956. The day before, Grimond had made a powerful speech which ensured that the leadership would be coming to someone with every intention of giving the Party direction and purpose. One of his major problems as leader was restoring a sense of identity. It was a problem always present and compounded by the narrow front strategy which obliged the Party to give advice to Liberals upon how to vote in seats where no Liberal was standing. In 1955 contradictory advice came from different quarters of the Party; some, such as Lord Moynihan, urging Liberals to vote Conservative, while others urged them to vote Labour. The 1955 election was also followed by further defections, Dingle Foot, a former MP, joining Labour and Lord Moynihan joining the Conservatives. These defections were evidence of a problem which went right to the heart of the question of the Party's future. It was not only a matter of holding on to existing activists and supporters, tempted by the opportunities in larger parties to put some part of their credo into action, but also of appealing to the less committed voters who were showing some signs of being ready to give the Party support in by-elections. One of the findings from local surveys carried out in the 1955 General Election was that the image of the Liberal Party remained unclear to the great mass of voters. Two impressions dominated: one was the unflattering but not altogether surprising view that the Liberal Party was 'finished'; the other was that the Party lay somewhere 'between' the Conservative and Labour Parties, as a compromise or centre party. It was the latter which was most prevalent among those who were likely to choose the Liberal Party to vote for.[2] Grimond's vigorous, fresh leadership would help to dispel the image of being defunct, but it was imperative that he also remedied its drift in policy terms. With many of its progressive clothes already stolen by Labour or by the more Liberal wing of the Conservatives and its place as a bastion against collectivism undermined by the Tories, the Liberals were in urgent need of a sense of direction. It was Grimond who was gradually to fashion the idea of the Liberal Party as a party of the radical, non-socialist left of centre, a position it has consistently returned to under a succession of leaders.

Grimond was fortunate to be coming to power just at a time when disenchantment with the Conservatives was beginning to offer opportunities to the Liberals. One of Grimond's first tasks as leader was to decide the Liberal stand on Eden's bungled Suez Operation. There was some division of opinion in the Party over the propriety of the initial action, reflected in three Liberals voting in support of the Conservative Government's ultimatum to Egypt on 30 October 1956, but two days later Liberal members voted with Labour deploring the invasion. On 2 November the Liberal Party issued a condemnation of the Government's Suez policy, endorsed four days later by the Liberal Parliamentary Party.

Suez notwithstanding, the first by-election test of the Liberals under Grimond was not auspicious. Carmarthen was fought in February 1957 as a straight fight with Labour, but it was Labour who proved the beneficiaries of the Conservative Party's discomfiture over Suez. It was a double blow. The successful candidate was the former Liberal Lady Megan Lloyd George, a cruel reminder of the long-running story of defections from the Party, as well as reducing Liberal representation to five seats. But 1957 saw a string of by-elections in which Liberal candidates managed to win an encouraging percentage of the votes cast, including over 36 per cent of the vote in North Dorset. The trend of these by-elections was of the Party taking a significant proportion of the protest vote against an unpopular Conservative Government. Gallup polls late in 1957 showed the Conservatives recording their lowest ratings since 1951 and the Liberals breaking into double figures for the first time since February 1952. Although insufficient to win any of the seats, the Liberal party was beginning to experience a phenomenon which was to remain a feature of the third-party challenge thereafter: the ability to obtain a higher percentage of the vote in by-election contests than in general elections and significantly higher than the routine polls taken by Gallup and other polling organizations.

The Liberal Party entered 1958 on a Gallup Poll rating of 10 per cent against 33 per cent for the Conservatives and 39 per cent for Labour. At the by-election in Rochdale in February 1958 the Liberals achieved one of their best performances since the war. Fought by the television presenter Ludovic Kennedy, a lively campaign achieved 35.5 per cent of the vote, 4,500 behind Labour and pushing the defending Conservatives into third place on just under 20 per cent. The next by-election at Torrington in March saw the Liberals buoyed up by their previous success, the Gallup poll at the end of February giving them 15 per cent against the defending Conservatives' 28 per cent, the best poll rating for the Party since 1945. At Torrington on 27 March, Mark Bonham-Carter achieved for the Liberals their first by-election victory since 1929. It was narrowly won, by a margin of only 658 votes, but it was a critical success for a Party which had been starved of good news for so long. Special factors could be adduced for the victory: it was a seat which had not been fought by the Liberals in 1955 and there was a residual Liberal tradition in the West Country for the Party to tap. On a raised turnout, the Liberals had capitalized on voters who had abstained in the 1955 election and had won over some Conservative support. However it was obtained, the result was a tremendous boost to morale. But it remained for some time an isolated victory rather than the beginning of a major breakthrough. The Party secured respectable and encouraging performances in by-elections through the rest of 1958 and into 1959, gathering around a quarter of the votes cast, but no further seats were won. In fact, the Torrington by-election was soon to reveal another feature of later Liberal revivals which was that individual victories could not always be translated into a major and sustained increase in seats in the subsequent general elections.

The general election called in October 1959 was seen most visibly as a stuggle between Labour and the Conservatives; a new Conservative Premier with strong populist tendencies attempting to fend off a respected Labour challenger, Hugh Gaitskell. The Conservatives won a convincing victory, their third in a row with 365 seats against Labour's 258. The Liberals had entered the election boosted by the Torrington victory, with a reasonably healthy financial situation and 216 candidates. The

Party returned six members, the same as in 1955 and 1951; there was no great new haul of seats and Torrington was lost. But the Party had raised its share of the vote to 5.9 per cent and the average vote per candidate was the highest since 1945. Also encouraging was the small number of lost deposits, at 56 the smallest since 1935.

Orpington and after

In the aftermath of the 1959 election, the Party received encouragement from a respectable third place in a by-election in Bolton East in 1960, when the Liberals decided to break the pact which had held since 1951, and a good performance at Paisley in April 1961 when they came within 2,000 votes of victory. During 1961–2 the Liberals achieved second place in eight by-elections. The disarray of the Labour Party was an undoubted factor; Labour was in the throes of its debate over unilaterialism in 1960–1 with Gaitskell seemingly at bay against his opponents. The Conservatives, too, were coming under fire for their 'complacency', especially in the face of growing balance of payments problems. The Gallup polls for 1961–2 showed the Liberals consistently achieving over 10 per cent with both Labour and the Conservatives occasionally falling as low as 30 per cent. In November 1961 the Liberals touched 14.5 per cent, almost matching their highest post-war poll rating at the time of the Torrington by-election. The good ratings held through the winter and in March 1962 the Liberals achieved the second great by-election breakthrough of the Liberal revival, the capture of Orpington on 14 March when Eric Lubbock overturned a Conservative majority of 14,760 and swept to a comfortable majority of 7,855 votes. A collapse in Conservative support had secured one of the most sensational by-election victories of the century.

To many, it appeared that the Party had at last made a crucial breakthrough, more so even than Torrington. The pro-Liberal tide seemed to be flowing strongly, especially in natural Conservative territory. Orpington was a middle-class commuter suburb of Kent, not one of the traditional Liberal areas of the Celtic fringe or the West Country. The victory, following a narrow miss in the solid Conservative seat of Blackpool North, seemed to promise the possibility of reaping a harvest of disillusioned Conservative support. One opinion poll at the end of March had the Liberals as the most popular party in the country, fractionally ahead of both Conservatives and Labour. Gallup, more conservatively and perhaps more accurately, gave the Liberals 22 per cent in their April poll, some distance behind Labour (35 per cent) and the Conservatives (29 per cent), but still their best Gallup rating by far since 1945. The Liberal tide washed through a series of by-elections; at Middlesbrough East, on the same day as Orpington, the Liberals forced the Conservatives into third place; In April the Party polled over a quarter of the votes at Stockton-on-Tees and achieved a similar result at Derby North. Further encouraging results in late spring and early summer had an important by-product in July: a major Cabinet re-shuffle in the Tory Government – Macmillan's 'Night of the Long-knives' – in which seven Cabinet ministers lost their posts. It was an important moment in post-war history in which Liberal by-election successes acted as a signal to an incumbent government that it required a drastic overhaul of personnel and policies.

The Liberal surge also saw important municipal gains for the Party after the trough of the 1950s. Compared with the miserly total of councillors elected in the mid-fifties the figure for elected councillors rose approximately fourfold to 196 in 1962. Moreover, like Orpington, the Liberals gained municipal seats in a fairly wide segment of southern and middle-class England. Less impressive, however, was the Liberal Party's ability to carry out Jo Grimond's hope of replacing the Labour Party with a non-socialist radical party. There was an obstinate failure to break into Labour territory whether in the London boroughs or in Labour's industrial heartlands. More worrying still was the evidence that by the autumn of 1962 public support was ebbing away. As the two major parties shaped up to fight the next general election and Labour's support began to rise to new heights, Liberal support fell. By the end of 1963 the Party was once again registering under 10 per cent in the polls; the days of Orpington already seemed far away. By-election performances also proved disapointing. In spite of Grimond's renewed appeal in June 1964 to a classless society, *Charter for New Men*, the party entered the 1964 election contest on a downward drift in its support. The Liberals fielded 365 candidates, but secured the election of only nine MPs. The results were widely seen as a disappointment. 'Orpington man' had failed to deliver a decisive vote to the Liberals. Indeed, the evidence of Labour's very narrow victory over the Conservatives and Home's remarkable feat in limiting the proportions of Labour's victory, suggested that the majority of Orpingtom men and their wives had probably voted Conservative. The seats the Party had gained read like a roll-call of *traditional* Liberal territory; Bodmin in the West Country and three seats in the North of Scotland. The breakdown of the pacts in Bolton and Huddersfield, so important for the Party's survival in the 1950s, saw both seats lost. But there were compensating signs of advance. The Party had raised its share of the vote to 11.2 per cent and there were more than three million Liberal voters, in both cases the best performance since 1929. Moreover, all its candidates had been elected in three-cornered contests without benefit of pacts or special arrangements. The average Liberal share of the vote per candidate was now 18.5 per cent, back to the level of 1945, and the number of lost deposits was only 53. The great prize of the recent Liberal revival, Orpington, was retained, unlike Torrington in 1959. In fact, the party had polled quite well in suburban areas even though it had failed to take any seats.

The difficulty for the Party was that Labour's victory seemed to postpone yet again the prospect of a realignment of the left brought about by the break-up or irremedial failure of Labour to secure a victory for the fourth time in a row. Even with a precarious overall majority of four, Labour was clearly in the saddle and in no mood to contemplate deals with the Liberals. Although its performance was greatly improved, the Liberal Party was no nearer to a controlling voice in politics than in the recent past. Grimond's sounding out of the possibilities of co-operation with Labour in an interview with the *Guardian* was met with deafening silence from Labour, division within the Parliamentary Party and outright hostility from the Liberal Assembly. Denounced by Nancy Sear for 'a-whoring after foreign women', Grimond was forced to steer clear of such ideas. As far away from power as ever, the slide in Liberal fortunes continued through the intervening period between the 1964 and 1966 elections. During 1965 the Party's Gallup poll ratings were consistently under 10 per cent and on the eve of the March 1966 General Election were as low as 5 per cent. A string of poor by-election performances also suggested that the days of revival were past, the only bright spot being David Steel's victory at Roxburgh, Selkirk and Peebles in March 1965. The Party entered the election campaign of 1966 with nothing like the same optimism as in 1964, its best hope being to hold the balance of power if the result was as close as 1964. Only 311 candidates were put forward, 54 less than two years earlier and three-quarters of them attacking Conservative-held seats. In one sense the result was a success; the party took 12 seats, raising its representation in the Commons to its highest point since the war. Although there was a fall in the overall Liberal vote and a dip in the vote secured per candidate, the Party might have been satisfied with a modest improvement in its fortunes. But the improvement was obtained in the context of a Labour triumph – a huge 97-seat majority which ended any possibility of deals with the Labour Party. There was another, more worrying feature. This was the revival of Scottish and Welsh Nationalist Parties. Plaid Cymru had put forward a score of candidates in 1959, 1964 and 1966. Although its total vote was small, it was recording a steady 8 or 9 per cent average vote for its candidates. In Scotland, the Scottish National Party raised its candidature from five in 1959 to 20 in 1966, its candidates winning only a marginally smaller share of the vote on average than the Liberals. There was a real danger, soon to become apparent, that the Liberals would be challenged in the very areas which they had relied upon to maintain some kind of electoral base. The Nationalists, too, threatened to outflank the Liberals on one of the issues on which they could claim some kind of distinctiveness, devolution and regional government. If these issues were being promoted as actively by the Nationalists, particularly if they could obtain some MPs, then the Liberal claim to be the third party in Wales and Scotland, possibly even in Britain as a whole, might be threatened.

More widely, it was apparent that the Party still lacked a clear identity for many voters, its capacity to act as a vehicle for protest not yet matched by its ability to project a distinctive, positive image at a general election in competition with the other main parties. Almost in recognition of this, Jo Grimond resigned as leader in 1967 with many commentators arguing that his dream of a radical alternative to Labour had, in fact, failed to materialize. The paradox was that where the Liberals seemed best able to capture new votes was as an alternative middle-class vote in suburban Tory-held seats – it remained an almost total failure in its assault on Labour-controlled areas.

The Thorpe era

The new leader in 1967 was Jeremy Thorpe. Once again the Party had chosen a young leader, only 38. Educated, like Grimond, at Oxford he was a trained lawyer and a talented television and media performer. But the late 1960s brought an even younger generation of Liberals to the fore. One by-product of the student activism of the decade was an infusion of radical young people into the Party. The Young Liberals began a pronounced leftward trend which caused considerable discomfort for the staid, older generation of Liberals. As an example, in 1966 the Young Liberals were demanding the withdrawal of all American troops from Vietnam; workers' control of nationalized industries; non-alignment in the Cold War; British withdrawal from Nato; opposition to the wage freeze; support for majority rule in Rhodesia; and active support for the anti-apartheid movement. But besides causing a certain amount of internal party strife, there were some lasting results. The Young Liberals placed increasing emphasis on what was known as 'community politics'; direct-action campaigns and support for local issues even of the most banal kind, sometimes dubbed 'pothole and pavement' politics, provided an outlet for activists. It brought the Liberals into the forefront of one of the most potent socio-political movements of the late sixties and early seventies, the development of grass-roots organizations such as tenants' groups, community associations and conservation lobbies. The growth of these forces was part of a growing disillusionment with the excesses of bureaucracy and the crassness of planning, increasingly highlighted by the housing and redevelopment boom of the sixties and early seventies. At the local level Liberals were also able to take advantage of the decay and complacency of the major parties, particularly in urban areas. The 'Focus' leaflet and community newsletter became one of the hallmarks of local campaigning. An important result of this was that the Liberals began to build up a strong cohort of local councillors on the basis of community issues. Less relevant to their success were traditional Liberal policies or even the fervent anti-apartheid and anti-Vietnam War causes espoused by the Young Liberals. What they offered was genuine local represen-tation of a kind that many areas had not enjoyed for some time. The new style of politics was particularly successful in decayed and moribund Labour territory in the big cities, Liberals building up a council base in cities such as Liverpool, Leeds and Birmingham. Its importance, however, lay beyond local town halls. By bringing in a new generation of recruits to the Party it added a fresh layer of activists to the 'old' Liberals still closely identified with the Party's traditional base in the Non-conformist churches. Above all, community politics appeared to work not only in securing the election of Liberal councillors, but also in building up a strong basis from which to challenge for parliamentary seats. The proof of this came in June 1969, when in one of the areas heavily worked on by Liberal community politics, Birmingham Ladywood, the Liberals achieved an im-portant by-election victory, the first for four years.

The Liberals entered the seventies and the prospect of another general election with mixed fortunes. Much of the late sixties had been dominated by the struggle to contain the radicalism of the Young Liberals, culminating on 31 January 1970 with a vote of censure by the Party's National Executive 'requesting' the Young Liberals to dismiss their Chairman Louis Eaks. Although this drew a not unexpected hostile reception from Young Liberals, the succession of Tony Greaves as Chairman at the Skegness Young Liberal Conference had to some extent eased the situation. In spite of Birmingham Lady-wood, the by-election record as a whole was not promising, with some poor results and the party's poll ratings remaining stuck in single figures from June 1969, touching 5 per cent in January 1970. Party finances were again in a parlous state with a six-figure overdraft at the bank. According to the Party treasurer, Sir Frank Medlicott, more than four-fifths of the Party's election funds in 1970 came from only 25 people.

The 1970 General Election was later described by the subsequent leader of the Party, as a 'disaster'.[3] The Party's number of MPs was halved, to six. The share of the vote also fell to 7.5 per cent, the absolute number of votes at just over two million was a third less than in 1964 and the vote per candidate was less than at any time since 1950. Seats were lost every-where; the recent by-election gain at Birmingham Ladywood, the former great prize of Orpington, the recently-won seats in Cheadle and Colne Valley, as well as Bodmin in the West Country and two seats in Scotland. The trail of lost deposits was a long one, 184 in all, the highest since 1950. There was no obvious sign of encouragement; indeed there was a particularly serious cloud on the horizon: the continued rise of the National-ist parties. In July 1966 Plaid Cymru had made their own by-election breakthrough at Carmarthen; in November 1967 the Scottish National Party had done the same at Hamilton. These successes produced an all-out effort in 1970. Plaid Cymru put up 36 candidates contesting every Welsh constitu-ency and securing 175,000 votes. Although no candidate was elected they had polled little short of the Liberals for each candidate in Wales. The Scottish Nationalists trebled their candidature to 65, obtained almost 307,000 votes and secured one MP. In Scotland and Wales, the Liberals were faced with the prospect of their own topsy-turvy fortunes and a potential decline in their seats being met by a rising tide of Nationalist MPs.

With the parliamentary scene so bleak, the only alternative was to build upon the base of community politics fashioned in the late 1960s. At the 1970 Party conference a Young Liberal resolution proposing that the Party should start campaigning and working at community level was adopted. Indeed, it was only at local level that the Party had any successes to boast. Most spectacular were the local election results in Liverpool where Trevor Jones led the local Party from representation by a solitary councillor in 1968 to becoming the largest single group on the Council in 1973. The importance of this new force was recognized at the 1972 Liberal Assembly when Jones became President of the Party. Moreover, as the Conservative Government began to run out of steam, the Liberals were able once again to achieve by-election success. Cyril Smith won Rochdale in October 1972 with a majority of just over 5,000 from Labour. A large personal vote for Smith was assisted by a strong presence at local level which allowed the Liberals to sweep up the Conservative vote as the main challenger to Labour. At Sutton and Cheam in December, the Liberals secured a 'second Orpington', overturning a 7,500 majority in commuterland. Both of these successes owed a great deal to the strength of Liberals on the ground and to the practice of community politics. The lesson was rammed home by an abject failure at Uxbridge on the same day as the Sutton and Cheam by-election where the Liberals lost their deposit. Good by-election performances elsewhere, some of them in Labour territory, confirmed that by 1973 a new Liberal revival was under way. Once again the Party's poll ratings climbed safely into double figures, reaching as high as 22.5 per cent in the Gallup poll for August. But the latest revival also registered more solid gains in local government. The Liberals were beginning a process which was to carry them through the seventies as a force in local politics. Liverpool was not an isolated breakthrough. By 1974 the Liberals had become the largest party in five authorities and taken power at Eastbourne. In another score of councils the result was that the Liberals were either the major opposition or the second largest party. Impressive in absolute terms, these figures still represented only a fraction of the total council seats available; in large parts of the country, especially in the GLC and the big conurbations, Liberals still only had a minor role to play. The revival of 1973 was confirmed with two by-election successes at Ripon and the Isle of Ely on 26 July. Ripon was almost a classic community politics campaign led by David Austick; Ely, a traditional Liberal area won by the well-known television personality, Clement Freud. Alan Beith's victory at Berwick-on-Tweed in November, Beveridge's old seat, confirmed a year of success.

When Heath called a snap election in February 1974 in the midst of the 'three-day week' and the miners' strike, he did so at a propitious time for the Liberals, going into an election with a revival in full-swing. This was reflected in the largest field of Liberal candidates since 1906, 517 in all. With Labour positively gloomy about its prospects, the Liberals anticipated some improvement on the 1970 result. In terms of the absolute number and share of the vote, the Party achieved a major success; over six million votes, nearly a fifth of all votes cast and four million up on 1970. In percentage terms it was the best Liberal result since 1929 and, in fact, more people had voted Liberal than at any previous election. But, as in 1929, the tally of seats gained was meagre, very much so, a harsh reflection of the truth that in percentage terms any share of the vote under 30 per cent was likely to leave the Liberals recording relatively few gains. The six million plus votes brought only 14 seats. Old losses were recaptured, including Colne Valley, Bodmin, and Hazel Grove (the former Cheadle); majorities in seats only narrowly held in 1970, like David Steel's Roxburgh, were strengthened; and some by-election successes retained and new gains made, such as the Isle of Wight. In spite of the huge candidature, there was only a score of lost deposits, Liberal candidates averaging some 23 per cent. The overall outcome in terms of seats was disappointing, however, and anyone looking at the regional figures could see confirmation of worrying trends. The threat of the Nationalist parties rivalling the Liberals in Celtic Britain was now made manifest. On the same date as the Liberal triumph at Berwick in November 1973 the SNP had taken Glasgow Govan. In February 1974 they put up

70 candidates of whom seven were elected. Plaid Cymru had put up 36 and gained two seats. With only three Liberals elected in Scotland, it was the SNP which was now the third party in Scotland. In Wales too, the two Welsh Nationalists matched the two Liberals elected. A pessimistic scenario could easily be conjured up in which the Liberals made a scatter of gains in England, while their potential to gain a substantial proportion of seats in the Celtic fringe was eroded by the growing strength of the Nationalists.

But the outcome of the election was overshadowed by the prospect that the Liberals might achieve a share in power by supporting the Tory Government of Edward Heath. Although the Tories had lost 33 seats compared with 1970, they were still only five seats behind Labour. The situation hoped for by Grimond in 1966 now beckoned as Heath opened talks with Thorpe about the possibility of a coalition to preserve his Government in power. Although Heath offered Thorpe a seat in the Cabinet, he was unable to offer more than the prospect of a Speaker's Conference on proportional representation rather than a firm commitment to electoral reform. There was also a strong feeling within the Liberal Party that 'propping up' a government which had lost its majority at an election of its own choosing was hardly likely to impress the millions of those who had voted Liberal against Heath's Government. After a weekend of negotiations within the Liberal Party and two meetings between Thorpe and Heath the chance of a deal slipped away and a minority Labour Government was formed.[4] The hope of a share in power and the prospect of electoral reform was as distant as ever. Labour, as in 1964, was in no mood for a coalition with the Liberals, seeking to survive long enough to convert its unexpected chance of government into a clear majority.

Although the prospect of a 'hung' Parliament had been widely canvassed in the press prior to the election, the reality when it came caught the Liberals unprepared. Thorpe had, initially, been more satisfied with what was on offer than many of his colleagues. What Liberal priorities were in such a situation and how strong their commitment was to proportional representation emerged as a dilemma which was to dog the Party through successive election campaigns. Some argued that the Party should refuse coalition in any circumstances and wait until it gained power in its own right, but it threatened the prospect of permanent or at least long-term exile from government. The alternative of accepting coalitions with other parties was potentially attractive, but also raised the thorny question of what policies were to form the basis of any arrangement. These debates rumbled on in the Party during the interlude between the two elections of 1974 with clear differences of opinion opening up between the National Executive and the leadership. The former, for example, resolved that the Liberal Party would 'not join a coalition with the Conservative or Labour parties separately and will make this clear at the next election'. This was flatly in contradiction to what Party spokesmen such as David Steel had said in party political broadcasts. The issue was only patched up at the Liberal Assembly in September 1974 when it was agreed that a meeting of the Party council would be held prior to any final decisions being taken on post-election deals with other parties. Although these restrictions were viewed with some impatience by MPs, they were indicative of tensions and suspicions between some of the activists in the country and the Party leadership in London. The second General Election of October 1974 removed the immediate prospect of this division coming into the open when Labour secured a small overall majority. In spite of fielding over 100 more candidates than in February, the total Liberal vote fell back to 5,300,000 and the share of the vote to just under 19 per cent. The number of MPs was trimmed back to 13. As significant, the Nationalist challenge was now fully realized. The SNP won 11 seats and Plaid Cymru three. In practice, the Liberal revival of 1973–4 had bottomed out with the Party once again lacking clear opportunity either to exercise influence or to increase its popular support.

Immediate concern after the election was concentrated on the Common Market referendum of 1975. Liberal support for the Common Market had been one of its most consistent policies and Liberals like David Steel, now Foreign Affairs spokesman, played a prominent part in the successful 'Yes' campaign. There was some significant fall out: Steel found himself frequently sharing platforms with Roy Jenkins and other pro-marketeers of similar persuasion to himself; Steel also confessed himself to be impressed with the professionalism and resources which experienced campaigners from the other parties were able to bring to bear. The gap between the amateur efforts of the Liberals and what a well-funded professional machine could do, reinforced Steel's growing concern that the Party still had a long way to travel to match the other organizations.[5] Not least, Steel himself became a much more visible public figure, emerging from the backstairs job of Chief Whip negotiating between a notoriously squabblesome Party in the country and the leadership at Westminster as an attractive public performer.

The Steel leadership

Steel's high public profile was to be a major asset to him when in early 1976 the Party was rocked by allegations surrounding Jeremy Thorpe. Allegations of homosexual conduct, attempts to pay-off, frighten and even murder a man who claimed to be a former lover of Thorpe produced the largest press scandal since the Profumo affair. It also seriously undermined the Party's carefully built-up reputation for probity and high principle. The affair was ultimately to lead to the trial of Thorpe and others in April 1979 on charges of conspiracy to murder and incitement to murder, at which Thorpe was found not guilty on all counts. But long before that time, press speculation and allegations had destroyed Thorpe's leadership and with it the last glimmers of the Liberal revival of 1972–3. Thorpe resigned the leadership in May 1976. Following an interregnum leadership by Jo Grimond, Steel was elected leader in July in a contest with John Pardoe through the operation of a newly-devised and complicated electoral college giving the membership a deciding vote in the choice of leader – the first leader of a British political party to be elected by democratic means. Steel's election as a fresh, young leader with an impeccable reputation laid aside as much of the effects of the Thorpe affair as was possible as far as the

Party was concerned, but it did not prevent further press revelations which continued to affect the Party's public image until the acquittal of Thorpe in spring 1979.

Amidst the fall out of the Thorpe affair, Steel struggled to give the Party some direction after a period of almost unparalleled and damaging publicity. Behind Steel's boyish, clean-cut image, there was a determination to make the Party a more responsible and credible political organization. Notoriously impatient with the indiscipline of the existing Party structure, he had not been leader for more than a few weeks when he made his position clear in an interview with the *Guardian* that the Party had to 'start by getting a toe-hold on power which must mean some form of coalition'. When these views formed part of his first Assembly speech in Llandudno, Steel was greeted by open dissent from some of the delegates, but it was clear in which direction he intended to move.

Steel's strategy of avoiding the confusion of February 1974 by an open recognition that a pact or coalition ought to form part of the Party's movement towards power soon had its opportunity. By early 1977 the administration of the new Labour leader, Jim Callaghan, had seen its majority whittled away by by-election defeats, resignations and defections. It was also faced with mounting economic problems and mired in a slow-moving devolution Bill for Wales and Scotland. Threatened with a Conservative no-confidence motion, Steel and Callaghan agreed to the formation of the 'Lib-Lab Pact'. With the support of the Liberal MPs, Steel agreed to support the Labour Government in return for a consultative role on all aspects of government, but without seats in Cabinet or any firm promise of electoral reform. Its first result was the defeat of the no-confidence motion tabled by the Tories by 322 votes to 298. The terms of the Pact were formally announced on 23 March 1977 in a joint press statement. Its most concrete proposals were that the Government would press ahead with devolution legislation and find extra time for a Liberal housing Bill to deal with the question of the homeless. Many Liberals believed a better deal could have been struck – above all the provisions on electoral reform, even for the forthcoming European elections, were very vague. In spite of sometimes bitter criticism from the Party in the country and a loss of support, Steel defended the Pact in September on the consistent line he had argued since the mid-seventies, that the Pact prepared the way for a break with the antagonistic two-party duopoly and that a Party which stood for proportional representation could not shy away from the opportunity of co-operation when it arose under the existing arrangements. In reality, as Steel was only too ready to point out, the Liberals had less to bargain with than they thought. Callaghan's alternative was to go to the country. The Liberal position in the opinion polls was now well down into single figures with a string of by-election failures behind them – no seat had been won since Berwick in November 1973 – and the results of an election for the Liberals would almost certainly prove disastrous. Although the Party made brave noises about leaving the Pact when the vote for proportional representation for the European Parliament was lost in the Commons, Steel pointed to the almost total lack of public interest in the issue. Matters were tense enough, however, for Steel to have to threaten his own resignation. The Pact only survived by a slender margin on a vote of the Parliamentary Party just before Christmas 1977 and after a successful defence of it at a special conference in Blackpool in January 1978. But by the end of May 1978, the Pact was over. The passage of the devolution Bills and the prospect of a forthcoming general election forced both parties to enter a pre-election period untrammelled by cross-party arrangements.

Although the Party had gained little tangible from the Pact and many still felt it had been a mistake, there was little doubting that Steel had played a difficult hand well. He had survived considerable dissent within the Party and earned a resounding victory at the special conference in January 1978. By not being afraid to put his leadership at stake, he had emerged with some authority from the first genuine experiment in coalition govenment since the war. On the other side of the equation, however, it was easy for critics to allege that the Pact ensured that the Liberal Party was tainted with the failures and unpopularity of the Labour Government. As the Party prepared for an autumn 1978 election, it was not in a strong position. In four of the last six months of 1978, the Party stood at only 4.5 per cent in the Gallup polls. Callaghan's postponement of a general election until the following year and the ensuing 'Winter of Discontent' left the Liberals with little prospect of a fresh rallying of support. The one chink of light was a startling good by-election result at Liverpool Edge Hill on 29 March 1979, virtually on the eve of the general election. Symptomatic of what was to come the Labour vote collapsed, giving David Alton a clear victory. Liverpool was one of the strongest centres for Liberal community politics. The question was whether the Liberals could transfer this kind of support into a country-wide campaign.

The Liberal manifesto in 1979 had been prepared with 1978 in mind. Its four main issues were political reform, industrial and economic reform, tax reform and the environment. Direct proposals included electoral reform, a Freedom of Information Act, a reformed second chamber to replace the Lords, a Bill of Rights and devolution to the English regions as well as to Wales and Scotland. Having persuaded the Labour Government during the Lib-Lab Pact to add a profit-sharing scheme to the 1978 Finance Bill, the Liberals proposed further extension of such schemes to promote industrial partnership. Another policy initiative was a switch from direct to indirect taxation. The Liberals also wanted to abolish the domestic rating system and institute a statutory prices and incomes policy. With growing concern about pollution and energy shortages – the Ecology Party had been founded in 1975 – the Party also wanted to institute energy conservation measures.

This was a reasonably coherent and in many ways a forward-looking manifesto. The *Economist* called it 'strikingly the best party manifesto'. Several of its items would be borrowed by the Labour Party or the Tories in the course of the next ten years. The difficulty was that the tide flowing against Labour was very strong and it was easy for the Conservatives to label the Liberals as part authors of the country's misfortunes for their role in the Lib-Lab Pact. Whatever disclaimers Steel could try to provide, those seeking a clear alternative to the Labour Government had a ready-made opportunity in the fresh and abrasive tone of Mrs Thatcher's Conservative Party. None the less, the Liberals fielded 577 candidates and ran an effective campaign in which Steel proved an impressive television performer who generated some momentum for the Party during the campaign's later stages. Women voters, in particular, were proved subsequently to have been prepared to shift their voting intentions to the Liberals.[6] The results, however, were disappointing. With some Conservative newspapers openly concerned about a Liberal surge against an unpopular Labour Government and perhaps still wary of an untried Conservative leader, the Conservatives had in fact won a convincing victory and a clear majority. The Liberals had lost another million votes; down to 4,313,000 with only 11 MPs elected. The share of the vote was 13.8 per cent and the average vote per candidate 14.9 per cent. In both respects these were a substantial fall on the October 1974 result. The toll of lost deposits was huge, 284, the highest total since 1950. Prospects of holding the balance of power and talk of alliances or pacts were now a dead letter; similarly, the hopes of the Liberals in the 102 constituencies where the Liberals had come second in October 1974 were dashed by a performance which was generally depressed. The losses were also high-profile ones: Thorpe lost his North Devon seat, gamely, some felt foolheartedly, braving the inevitable problems of an impending trial; so did John Pardoe, the defeated leadership contender.

There were some sources of comfort. Had it not been for the level of success enjoyed in 1974, the result would have been a good one. With over four and a quarter million voters, the Party had achieved more votes than in any other post-war election. Ther was still a large block of Liberal voters, something like a half of them first-time Liberal supporters. These two factors: a still substantial section of the vote, plus the ability to win over new supporters, were encouraging features. The Party could continue to boast that its numerical support was greatly under-represented in terms of the number of MPs reinforcing the case for electoral reform, while the ability to attract floating voters was one which promised the hope of revival in the future. Less obvious, but no less significant, was the collapse of the Nationalist challenge in Scotland and Wales following the failure of the referendums on Scottish and Welsh devolution. The SNPs storming success in October 1974, when it had gained 11 seats, was now firmly reversed, reducing it to only two. With three Scottish MPs, the Liberals were once again – by a whisker – the third party in Scotland. In Wales, too, the Nationalist advance was stemmed. Plaid Cymru's temporary hold on three seats was reduced to two, one ahead of the Liberals. Moreover, while fending off the challenge within the Celtic fringe, the results in 1979 offered some support for the view that the Party was at last broadening the geographical basis of its appeal. In every general election since 1945 up to 1979, more than half of the Liberal seats had been in Scotland, Wales and Devon and Cornwall. No less than 71 per cent of all election victories in general elections between 1945 and October 1974 occurred in these areas. In 1979, however, six of the 11 MPs came from outside the Celtic areas. In fact, the Party had also come second in 82 constituencies – a basis on which hope of future gains could be built. None the less, after more than 20 years since the Liberal revival became evident in the late 1950s, the Party was forced to take stock of a process which had left it with less than a dozen MPs and still far from the exercise of effective power.

The Liberal revival assessed

The Liberal revival of the period between the Torrington by-election and Mrs Thatcher's triumph has become something of a textbook cliché. But analysis of the nature of that revival reveals a series of different but sometimes overlapping processes. At least four different levels can be identified. The first was the build up of Liberal representation in Parliament from a low point in the 1950s of half a dozen seats to double figures by the 1970s. By 1979 it seemed unlikely that Liberal representation would fall back to the lower level, supported as it was by the second feature of the revival, the build up of the popular vote for the Liberals in general elections. Even if not always reaching the peak of February 1974, the Liberal revival had seen a substantial increase in the vote by the 1970s. Behind the rising Liberal vote at general elections lay not one revival but a series of surges in support shown in the poll ratings and usually marked by by-election successes. These pulses of revival were separated by distinct and almost predictable downturns, often taking support down to single figures in the polls. One peak of support was registered in late 1957 and the early part of 1958, marked by the Torrington by-election victory; the next came in 1962, continuing into 1963 – the 'Orpington revival'; another came in 1973, continuing into 1974. The peak of these revivals did not always coincide with general election campaigns; in fact, only the General Election of February 1974 was fought with a Liberal revival in full flow. But this revival, like the earlier ones, was spent by the mid 1970s, the Thorpe affair helping to push poll ratings down as low as single figures by late 1978. The 1979 election campaign may itself have seen the beginning of a new revival, signalled and assisted by the Edge Hill by-election of March 1979.

But the revival also operated on a third level. In municipal politics, the Liberal position was transformed over the period between the 1950s and the late 1970s. Although downturns in support also affected local representation, there was an overall increase in Liberal involvement in local government, far beyond what had been possible in the 1950s. While Liberals were still in a minority in most local councils even at the end of the 1970s, they had begun to be a force to be reckoned with in a wide variety of areas. Moreover, there was a relationship between Liberal involvement in local politics and national politics which was almost unique; areas where Liberals built up support on the basis of community politics were often turned into winnable parliamentary seats. Even if that had not been true, a key feature of the Liberal revival was the re-emergence of the Party at local level, one which could withstand downturns in the Party's national fortunes and provide some kind of ballast to the Parliamentary Party. As in all British parties, the elected MPs and councillors represented only the visible part of the iceberg of activists and Party members. Liberal survival had ensured that sufficient constituency organizations had maintained an existence to provide the foundation for later revivals. Quite where such survival ended and revival began was not always clear, but the process was often one of an overlap of traditional Liberal supporters with new activists. To a striking degree, traditions which had seemed broken were revived in areas and constituencies where Liberal support appeared dead. In Manchester, for example, the last Liberal councillors lost their seats in the 1950s, apparently bringing an end to a long Liberal tradition. A City Party remained in existence, however, and constituency organizations survived in places such as Manchester Withington, Ernest Simon's former seat, with its strong professional and university population, as well as run-down northern and central areas. As elsewhere, in Manchester Withington the Liberal flag was kept flying by stalwarts of local Nonconformist churches and a handful of 'old' Liberals. The accession of a younger group of activists assisted a revival in which one issue was establishing a conservation area for the central part of the constituency. By 1978 a local resident and leader of the local conservation campaign had been elected to the City Council, the first Liberal councillor for 20 years. Modest success was built on to produce a handful of Liberal councillors in Manchester by the early 1980s. This, in fact, was a more typical story of the local Liberal revival than the more spectacular municipal successes in places such as Liverpool, Eastbourne or Richmond. It represented successive layers of activity, often with rapid turnover, building on traditions and utilizing the remnants of existing organizations to fashion modest electoral success at local level. It often still meant derelict wards and whole constituencies, as well as an often fragile base in terms of numbers of activists and voters. But the standing joke of the other parties, that the biggest shock to many local Liberal candidates was that they might be elected, was beginning to wear thin by the end of the decade.

There was, however, a fourth aspect to the Liberal revival. As Party members and activists in the country were reminded in 1974 and again in 1977, the Parliamentary Party could find itself playing a role in government even with a small number of MPs. A close election result or the critical fall in a government's majority could give a third party like the Liberals a crucial role, subject only to the willingness of the larger parties to make terms which the Liberals could accept. The parliamentary situation and the strategy of the Liberal leadership were the major factors here. Both Thorpe and Steel, like Grimond before them, were not averse to deals with other parties, even on terms which some of the Party at large found too easy. Indeed, a feature of Steel's leadership was that he made obtaining a share in government as a first step to breaking the stranglehold of Labour and the Conservatives one of his primary objectives. A large number of MPs made participation in government more likely, but it was determined more by the direction given by the Liberal leadership, and crucially, the willingness of the other parties to open discussions. The closely-contested elections of February and October 1974 offered the Liberals greater bargaining power, especially as the Ulster Unionist bloc divided after 1970 and became detached from the old Unionist alliance with the Conservatives. Hence, in the critical and most public area of influence upon government, the Liberals had seen themselves twice in the 1970s close to power and, controversially in the Lib-Lab Pact, actually sharing it for the first time since the war-time coalition.

Underlying the wider aspects of Liberal revival were two related developments in voting behaviour. During the 1950s the two-party hegemony at general elections reached the highest point it was to achieve in the post-war era. In the general elections of 1951 and 1955 more than 18 votes in every 20 had been cast for the two major parties, a function of a very low Liberal candidature, but also of the apparently hopeless state of the Liberal cause. By the 1970s, the Liberals had prised apart the jaws of an apparently closing vice, raising their share of the vote to 7.5 per cent in 1970 and safely into double figures in the other three elections of the 1970s. The revival in the Liberal vote was part of a wider shift in political sociology during the period from the 1950s. Broadly speaking, the period saw a degree of dealignment from support for the two major parties which offered increasing opportunities for third parties like the Liberals. To an extent, there was cumulative disaffection from the major parties and the rise of both a greater floating vote and a greater readiness of the electorate to protest vote, expressing dissatisfaction with sitting governments two or three years into a Parliament. Both factors played an important part in the Liberal revival. The post-war period had opened with a Labour administration which seemed to embody much of the enthusiasm for change after the Second World War. By 1951 it had run out of steam and was replaced by the Tories. But by the latter part of the 1950s disillusion with both Conservatives and Labour offered the potential for the two mini-revivals of Torrington and Orpington. Labour's toe-hold on power in 1964 was followed by a sweeping victory in 1966 which, however, was to breed dissatisfaction in its turn. Once again the principal beneficiaries were the Conservatives, but when their Government ran into difficulties it offered renewed opportunities for the Liberals to reap a harvest of disaffected voters. By the mid-1970s there was a convincing case for arguing that both Labour and Conservatives had been tried and, in some important respects, had been found wanting. The eleven and a half million votes for the Liberals in the two elections of 1974 and the difficulties of either major party in securing an outright and convincing majority before 1979 suggested a significant role for other parties.

The ability of the Liberals to pick up both the floating and protest vote had been seen as a feature of the earliest revival of the Party's fortunes at the end of the fifties. It gave the Liberal revival particular characteristics which continued into the 1970s. One was a rapid turnover in support, much more so than in the other parties. Only 44 per cent of the 1959 Liberal voters remained loyal to the Party in 1964; only 38 per cent of those who did so in 1966 stayed with the Party in 1970; only half of those who voted Liberal in October 1974 did so again in 1979. In 1979 the figure for the Conservatives was 87 per cent and for Labout 75 per cent.[7] There was some evidence in the 1979 figure that the 'stickability' of the Liberal vote was improving, but its volatility was one of the features that was to remain into the era of Alliance politics; rapid and substantial accessions of support both at by-elections and general elections, much of which melted away in a short space of time. But another characteristic of this ability to attract a fluctuating body of voters was the broadening of the geographical and sociological basis of support. As we have seen, the Libral MPs of the 1970s were drawn from a wider geographical area than they had been between 1945 and 1970. Similarly, Liberal by-election successes were secured in all parts of the country, not just the Celtic fringe and there was ample evidence of the Liberals coming back into local government in many different parts of the country.

There was also evidence that there was something of a 'classless' appeal to the Liberals. As Geoffrey Alderman has noted, one of the characteristics of the Liberal revival was the remarkably even spread of support among different social classes.

Table 1 *Liberal Party preference by class, 1964–1979*, as a percentage of voters

	AB	C1	C2	DE
1964	15	14	11	9
1966	11	11	8	7
1970	10	9	7	6
1974 (February)	20	25	20	17
1974 (October)	22	21	20	16
1979	15	20	11	14

Data for 1964 – February 1974 from National Opinion Polls; for October 1974 from Harris; for 1979 from Gallup.
Source: Adapted from G. Alderman, *Modern Britain, 1700–1983*, (Croom Helm, London, 1986), p. 254.

The Liberals, then, were the beneficiaries of the breakdown of the stable class-based support of the major parties from the 1950s. This was confirmed by the British Election Studies which showed that, whereas in 1964 some 81 per cent of the electorate identified themselves with the Labour or Conservative parties, 40 per cent of them 'very strongly', from 1970, there was an erosion of this strong identification, down to 24 per cent of 'strong identifiers' by October 1974.[8] The lowering of the age of voting to 18 in 1969 also added cohorts of younger voters whose partisanship was traditionally less strong. But survey evidence also suggested that partisan commitments were weakening within the electorate as a whole. The media and election camapaigns themselves were beginning to have more impact than family and class background. There was evidence in 1979, for example, that effective Liberal party political broadcasts had helped to generate the late swing to the Party in the final stages of the campaign.[9]

The Liberals, then, could be seen as the beneficiaries of a changing political sociology. This was confirmed by the emergence of other forces in British politics at about the same time. The loosening of the dominance of the two major parties was seen in the rise of the Nationalist parties in Wales and Scotland, the divorce of the Northern Ireland Unionists from the Conservatives and their split into two groups voting independently in the Commons, the rise of the National Front as a contender in general and local elections, the challenge of new left-wing groupings and the founding of the Ecology Party in 1975. Although not all of these groups were able to elect MPs, or even councillors, they began to show a degree of support. By the February 1974 election there were 11 MPs other than Liberals and Northern Ireland MPs; in October 14. Although reduced to four in 1979, the share of the vote taken by other parties in both the 1974 and the 1979 elections was between 3 and 4 per cent. The list of those putting forward candidates included Communists, the Workers Revolutionary Party, Ecology, National Front and Scottish and Welsh Nationalists. They accounted in February 1974 for 324 candidates, 344 in October 1974 and 690 in 1979.

The Liberals managed only precariously to stay one step ahead in this race for third-party influence. In the mid-1970s the Nationalist successes deprived the Liberals of that position in Wales and Scotland, but it proved only temporary. The Liberals were the only party which could claim both a country-wide appeal and a sizeable group of MPs through the 1970s. As before, the Liberals were beneficiaries as much as the victims of the first-past-the-post system in contest with other small parties outside Scotland and Wales. For example, although it was a threat which came to nothing, the National Front in the General Election of 1979 put up 303 candidates and polled 190,747 votes. In some parts of Britain a 'list' system of proportional representation for general and local elections might have given the National Front representation in the Commons and almost certainly given them a role in local government. As it was, only the regionally-based Nationalist parties proved capable in the 1970s of getting more than a single MP elected.

The Liberals remained after the 1979 election the only major third party in British politics, with a popular vote in millions, a respectable number of MPs and strong representation in local government. The Liberal 'revival', however, now more than twenty years old, still left them frustrated in their hope of exercising decisive influence. Prospects for parliamentary reform remained as insubstantial as they had been a generation earlier. Indeed, the election of a Conservative Government with the first safe majority since 1970 and one committed to a break with the Liberal Toryism of Heath, suggested that the route to power was decisevely blocked. Whatever its achievements, the Liberal revival seemed stalled.

Notes

1 See R.S. Milne and H.C. MacKenzie, *Marginal Seat, 1955*, (London, 1958), pp. 47–9.
2 *Ibid.*, pp. 135–6.
3 D. Steel, *Against Goliath: David Steel's Story*, (Weidenfeld and Nicolson, London, 1989), p. 66.
4 *Ibid.*, p. 78–81.
5 *Ibid.*, pp. 85–6.
6 J. Rasmussen, 'David Steel's Liberals: Too old to cry, too hurt to laugh', in *Britain at the Polls, 1979: A Study of the General Election*, in H.R. Penniman ed. (American Enterprise Institute, London and Washington, 1981), p. 170.
7 *Ibid.*, p. 171.

8   Cited in G. Alderman, *Modern Britain, 1700–1983*, (Croom Helm, London, 1986), p. 256.
9   For evidence of the late swing see J. Rasmussen, *op.cit.*, Fig. 5.1, p. 169.

5 The Age of Alliance, 1981–1987

The Conservative victory at the 1979 General Election was to mark the beginning of the most promising period for third-party politics for decades and appear, for a time at least, to offer the opportunity for a major realignment of politics. The formation of the Social Democratic Party in March 1981 was the most important breakaway of a group of MPs and senior figures from a major party since the War. The swift formation of an Alliance between the SDP and the Liberals created for the first time since 1945 a credible alternative third force contending for government. In the 1983 General Election, the Alliance was to come within a few percentage points of overtaking the Labour Party in the popular vote. But neither in 1983 nor in 1987 were the Alliance partners able to secure the breakthrough in seats required to achieve parity with the two other parties. Even before the 1987 General Election, the Alliance seemed to have been forced into permanent minor-party status. Realignment had failed to occur. Why it did so illustrated both particular failings on the part of the Alliance as well as unfavourable circumstances which affected any attempts to make third-party intervention more decisive. After the 1987 election, the high hopes of an Alliance breakthrough were gone, leading to the attempt to refashion the Alliance as a new third party.

The SDP and the Alliance

Mrs Thatcher's election victory in 1979 seemed to have broken the near stalemate of party politics since the mid-1970s by obtaining a clear majority for her brand of Conservatism. But on the left of centre, the effects of defeat were to bring to a head the strains within the Labour Party and the bitter conflicts between left and right. Two factors came together in the formation of the Social Democratic Party. One was a long-running campaign by a section of the Labour Party to achieve a realignment in British politics. Roy Jenkins, former deputy leader of the Labour Party, in his Dimbleby Lecture of 22 November 1979 argued the need for a new centre party with a programme of radical social and constitutional reform. The new party would seek to attract support from left and right, as well as those who had hitherto played little part in politics, alienated by the adversarial nature of the Labour-Conservative contest. Jenkins drew upon a tradition which had stretched back as far as Dick Taverne's short-lived career as a breakaway Democratic Labour victor in the Lincoln by-election in 1973 and ultimately to the Gaitskellite inheritance of a more broadly-based social democratic tradition which many felt was stifled by the Labour Party's close identification and constitutional entanglement with the trade union movement. The other factor was the increased leftward drift of the Labour Party. Discontent among Labour moderates was expressed even before the 1979 election defeat by the formation in 1977 of a centre-right pressure group, Campaign for a Labour Victory, founded by Ian Wrigglesworth, John Cartwright, William Rodgers and Alec McGiven. Although originally concerned with modernizing the Party, it was to become a vehicle for consideration of a breakaway from the Labour Party. As the Labour left began to exercise increasing influence on the party, the CLV began to make noises about the possibility of reforming a new democratic socialist party. The election of Michael Foot as leader, a long-standing supporter of unilateral nuclear disarmament, on 10 November 1980, marked a shift in the balance of power in the Party, followed by an acrimonious dispute over the method to be adopted for choosing the leader of the Party in future. The question of whether to adopt a 'one member, one vote' system, as opposed to the proposed electoral college system which gave a strong weighting to the trade unions, became the issue on which a group of MPs decided they could no longer stay within the Labour Party.

A week after the Special Labour Conference at Wembley in January 1981 reaffirmed the electoral college decision, the so-called 'Gang of Four' (Roy Jenkins, David Owen, William Rodgers and Shirley Williams) issued the Limehouse Declaration (25 January 1981) setting up an interim body called the Council for Social Democracy. Initially designated a pressure group rather than a separate party, the declaration attracted the support of nine Labour MPs. Events moved rapidly in the spring of 1981, with the Liberals under Steel giving encouraging support for the creation of a non-socialist alternative to Thatcherism. An opinion poll in the *Sun* gave a putative Liberal-Social Democratic arrangement 51 per cent of popular support; a hundred prominent people gave their backing to the Council for Social Democracy in an advertisement in the *Guardian* and called for funds and members; Shirley Williams resigned from Labour's National Executive and, on 2 March, 12 Labour MPs resigned the Party Whip. On 26 March the new Social Democratic Party was formally established, consisting initially of 14 MPs, 13 Labour and one Conservative. It was the largest defection of MPs from the Labour Party since 1931. Headed by a group of talented and experienced figures with Cabinet background it completely transformed in the short term the electoral position: at a step, the SDP became the third party in British politics.

Almost immediately the question of an alliance with the Liberals arose. The Liberals were already the beneficiaries of Labour's disarray and the growing unpopularity of the Conservative Government's hard-line monetarist economic policy, plunging Britian into its deepest recession since the War. In the May 1981 local elections, the Liberals recorded a net gain of 250 seats with the SDP not yet engaged as a national party. Actual discussions between the Liberals and the SDP proceeded informally: while Steel had close relations with Roy Jenkins, he had less direct links with the other members of the 'Gang of Four'. On the face of it, the formation of a separate SDP was something of a rebuff – why had the dissenting MPs not simply joined the Liberals? Here Jenkins' view that a separate party was the best interim vehicle for a realignment of British politics, bringing in hitherto uncommitted potential activists and voters, leading eventually to a merger, was not one necessarily shared by other members of the SDP. Dr Owen, in particular, was a strong supporter of the SDP's claim to a distinct identity and this difference in emphasis was one which was to bedevil relationships between the two groups over the next seven years. In the short term, however, a fortuitous opportunity came in April for Steel to consult with Shirley Williams and Bill Rodgers at the annual Anglo-German conference in Germany in April 1981. In what insiders called the 'Konigswinter Compact' the ground rules for the Alliance were laid, including the decision to issue a joint statement of principles, arrangements to conduct alternate by-elections as they arose and some kind of agreement on a share-out of constituencies in the event of a general election.

On 16 June the SDP and the Liberals issued a joint statement of policy, *A Fresh Start for Britain*. Its main proposals included parliamentary reform and proportional representation, a Freedom of Information Act, devolution, industrial partnership, support for Nato and continued EEC membership. These proposals were later to form the core of the parties' 1983 manifesto policies. Then in July 1981 the SDP had its first opportunity to test support when Roy Jenkins contested the Warrington by-election on 16 July. In a safe Labour seat where Liberals had hitherto only obtained a small vote, Jenkins came within 1,700 of victory. Although a defeat, Jenkins could rightly claim a moral victory for the new party. This encouraging result helped to provoke a strong and almost euphoric tide of support, for the prospects of 'breaking the mould' of British politics. At the Llandudno Liberal Conference in September, the unratified Alliance with the SDP received overwhelming support in an atmosphere which culminated in David Steel's address to the Assembly which ended with the words 'Go back to your constituencies and prepare for government'. The Alliance was then endorsed at the first SDP conference, a three-part event held in Perth, Bradford and London. Further defections from

Labour brought the total of SDP MPs to 21. On 22 October Bill Pitt for the Liberals secured the first of a series of spectacular by-election victories for the Alliance in Croydon North-West.

Breaking the mould

The acceleration of Alliance support was unprecedented, bringing a surge in third-party preference on a scale never seen before. In February 1981 just before the SDP was formed, the Liberals stood at 20 per cent in the opinion polls, against 36 per cent for the Conservatives and 35 per cent for Labour. By October, Gallup was polling 40 per cent for the Alliance, reaching an astonishing 50 per cent in December. With Labour in deepening disarray and the Thatcher premiership the most unpopular since opinion polling began, several opinion polls in the autumn and early winter of 1981 forecast a sweeping Alliance victory at a forthcoming general election. This tide of support was both translated into and reinforced by spectacular and headline-grabbing by-election victories, notably Shirley Williams at Crosby in November 1981 and Roy Jenkins at Glasgow Hillhead in March 1982. Williams converted an 18,000 plus Conservative majority into one of more than 5,000 votes for the SDP, a turnabout of massive proportions. Although Jenkins' victory at Hillhead was narrower, it confirmed the ability of the SDP to employ the same 'bandwagon' effect as the Liberals in their earlier revivals. Nor were the omens in local government any less propitious. In 214 municipal by-election contests between July and December 1981, Alliance candidates secured almost half the seats.

During the winter of 1981–2, then, it seemed that the Alliance could sweep all before it. There were, however, some problems emerging. The agreement concluded between the Liberals and the SDP to contest half of the parliamentary seats at the forthcoming election with the arrangements to be worked out at a regional level brought some tensions to the surface. Many Liberals had assumed that the SDP as a new party would contest a selection of seats, perhaps up to a hundred in the first instance. They were quickly disabused, finding that some SDP members were thinking seriously about contesting as many seats as possible. In that situation a 50-50 share out was the obvious compromise, but it was one bound to create problems at local level for the Liberals, many of whom would have to accept giving up to the SDP seats where Liberals had worked for years. These frictions were exacerbated by the nature of some SDP support at local level. Some Labour MPs and councillors who jumped ship to join the SDP did so because they were under pressure from the threat of deselection. Complaints from the Liberals that the local SDP were, in fact, some of their old enemies from local Labour politics in new guise, were met by SDP insistence that the Alliance bargain be held to. Other SDP newcomers to politics were also less than ready to yield primacy to Liberal candidates and organizations which claimed an established tradition, but often had very little electoral success to show for it. Negotiations over seat allocation between the two sides proved long, debilitating and time consuming. Just at the time when the Alliance and especially the SDP needed to strengthen its grass-roots organization, activists often spent hours on seat negotiations. Moreover, for a party like the Liberals, heavily dependent on relatively small numbers of activists, most of whom knew each other, there were real difficulties in keying into a party which was organized locally on a different basis to the Liberals, and which paid somewhat more attention to instructions from their headquarters than had ever been the case among the Liberal Party. Put in perspective these were minor irritants, greatly outweighed by the infusion of new supporters and activists, and with seemingly unlimited access to the media. But already, however, some of the publicity was not entirely favourable, with press reports of difficulties over the seat negotiations, especially after Bill Rodgers broke them off unilaterally at the start of the Christmas recess. Although attempts were made to smooth over the problems, not for the last time, the attempts to portray the Alliance as a unique and harmonious example of co-operation in British politics could be made to sound hypocritical and naive. These squabbles had some effect on the euphoric lead enjoyed by the Alliance in the polls between the Crosby and Hillhead by-elections; by early 1982 the lead had ben trimmed back to more like parity with the other parties.

Although this was still a remarkable showing, it was significant that the peak of Alliance support had already been passed when the fortunes of all parties, but especially the Conservatives, became bound up with the extraneous event of the Falklands conflict. On 2 March 1982 Argentinian forces invaded the Falkland Islands. A British task force was despatched to the South Atlantic on 5 April, recapturing South Georgia on 25 April and beginning air attacks on the Falklands on 1 May. On the 24th British troops went ashore at San Carlos leading to the eventual surrender of Argentine forces on 14 June. The effect of these events on Conservative support was dramatic; from a standing of 23 per cent in December 1981 when the Alliance was at its peak of 50 per cent, Conservative ratings rebounded to 46 per cent by July 1982 while Alliance support halved to 24 per cent. It was difficult not to attribute the almost complete about turn in the opinion polls to the 'Falklands factor', but, in fact, the slippage of Alliance support had already begun in early 1982 *before* the Falklands factor began to intervene.

There was evidence of a slow-down in Alliance support in the May 1982 local elections – the first national test of Alliance support. Overall results showed a level of support of 28 per cent, virtually in line with current poll ratings. But the two halves of the Alliance polled differently. More SDP seats were lost than gained as a result of defecting Labour councillors being defeated and the Liberals won nearly five times as many seats as the SDP. The overall results, however, were disappointing – the Alliance seemed set for a hard slog rather than the meteoric rise to power it had threatened only a few months earlier. By-elections told a similar story: the Alliance trailed in by-elections at Mitcham and Morden on 3 June, lost its deposit at Coatbridge and failed with the veteran Dick Taverne at Peckham. The Alliance had to wait until February 1983 for its next success, almost a year, when Simon Hughes secured Bermondsey with 58 per cent of the vote.

Table 2 *Voting intentions according to Gallup, March 1981–July 1982*

		Con %	Lab%	Alliance%
1981	Mar	30	34	32
	Apr	30	34	33
	May	32	35	29
	Jun	29	37	30
	Jul	30	40	26
	Aug	28	38	32
	Sep	32	36	29
	Oct	29	28	40
	Nov	26	29	42
	Dec	23	23	50
1982	Jan	27	29	39
	Feb	27	34	36
	Mar	31	33	33
	Apr	31	29	37
	May	41	28	29
	Jun	45	25	28
	Jul	46	27	24

The 1983 General Election proved that the Alliance, although capable of mounting the most successful third-party campaign in British post-war history, had been unable to 'break the mould' of British politics. The manifesto, *Working Together for Britain*, was well-received and contained a number of policies which firmed up previous Liberal positions on economic expansion, incomes policy and trade union reform. In the midst of record unemployment the Alliance promised a programme of economic expansion to create a million jobs over two years. Other policies included compulsory secret ballots for union elections, reform of the social security system, an incomes policy, continued membership of the Common Market, devolution to the regions and to Wales and Scotland and proportional representation. At the time of the dissolution, the Conservatives were securely in the lead in the polls. In spite of the high total of unemployed, the continued effects of the Falklands factor, a lowering of inflation and the greater prosperity of those in work gave the Conservatives a head start. Labour's manifesto was described by one Shadow Cabinet member as 'the longest suicide note in history'. It pledged the Party to leave the Common Market, adopt a non-nuclear policy, increase public expenditure and impose further nationalization. The result was a Conservative triumph on the basis of 42 per cent of the vote. Labour plummetted to its worst figure since 1918, to 28 per cent, while the Alliance showed a strong surge in the last few days of the campaign to end at just over 25 per cent. It was the best third-party showing since the 1920s, but it produced a meagre return in seats, only 23. Labour with only just over 2 per cent more of the vote had 209. The even spread of Alliance support meant that the seven and three quarter million votes for the Alliance were not translated into a share of seats in any way proportionate to its record poll for a third force. Labour, with less than three-quarters of a million more votes than the Alliance, had won 183 more seats. Where the Alliance had gained seats it had often been in those familiar parts of the country where the Liberal vote was most concentrated – Wales, the West Country and the Scottish borders. None the less, evidence of the wider geographical spread of support for the Alliance was shown in the ability to retain some of the by-election gains in England. The SDP tended to fare less well considered as a separate force. Only five of their sitting MPs survived and two of the former 'Gang of Four' – Shirley Williams and William Rodgers – lost their seats. There could be no question of holding the balance of power. The Conservatives had secured a crushing victory. Although there were some 44 MPs from outside the two main parties, the Conservatives still had an overall majority of more than 140 seats.

The mould unbroken?

The Alliance remained in a frustrating position between 1983 and 1987. While it consolidated its position in local government and was able to score occasional successes in parliamentary by-elections, its credibility as an alternative governing party remained in doubt. Moreover, David Owen's assumption of the leadership of the SDP in place of Roy Jenkins in 1983 created difficulties. A dominant personality both in the media and in Parliament, it was clear that Owen as well as having his own strong views on issues such as defence and economic policy, continued to take very seriously the idea of the SDP as an independent and distinct entity and was opposed to a merger with the Liberals. In spite of some success in making the Alliance a regular part of the political scene, during the summer and autumn of 1986 disagreements over defence policy threatened a major rift in the Alliance. The strong unilateralist and pacifist elements in the Liberal Party, only just held at bay by the leadership in previous years, were increasingly annoyed by what they saw as the pre-emption of nuclear policy by David Owen and apparent compliance by David Steel in discussion of a new generation of nuclear deterrent based on a 'Euro-bomb'. The resulting revolt of the Liberal Assembly at Eastbourne in September 1986, passing a non-nuclear amendment on defence policy in defiance of the party leadership, brought this rift into the open. Its effects on the standing of the Alliance in the opinion polls were felt almost immediately, demonstrating the vulnerability of Alliance support to disunity within its ranks. Although a compromise defence policy was patched-up by the New Year in time for a re-launch of the Alliance, the underlying tensions over defence and the dual leadership of the Alliance formed an undercurrent of concern about the ability of the Alliance to repeat and improve on its performance in 1983.

There were, however, optimistic signs. The build up of support at local level had continued. An increase in Alliance councillors meant that more councils either passed into Alliance control or, more usually, passed into a situation of no overall control. The by-election record also proved encouraging, particularly from the summer of 1986 when the Alliance secured a major success at Ryedale, almost on a par with the great triumphs at Orpington and Crosby, turning a 16,000 Conservative majority into an Alliance victory by 5,000 votes. The Alliance vote rose almost 20 per cent on 1983, collapsing the Conservatives and squeezing Labour. A near miss at West Derbyshire on the same day saw the Alliance vote rise by over 12 per cent to come within a hundred votes of victory. Although the nuclear debate in the autumn slowed down the Alliance bandwagon, there was evidence that the relaunch of the Alliance in January 1987 had allowed the momentum to be regained. The Greenwich by-election in late February 1987 was fought in less promising territory than either Ryedale or Derbyshire, but the SDP's candidate Rosie Barnes secured a resounding victory in what in 1983 had been a Labour-held seat with the Conservatives only 1,200 votes behind. The margin of victory, a 6,600 vote majority over Labour, with the Conservatives resoundingly beaten into third place, confirmed that a fresh Alliance revival was under way. It was followed in March 1987 by the successful Liberal defence in the Truro by-election, caused by the tragic death of the popular incumbent, David Penhaligan, in a car accident just before Christmas. The revival was reflected in several opinion polls in spring 1987 which showed the Alliance vying with Labour for second place and only a few points behind the Conservatives. On 27 March, 1987, Gallup actually had the Alliance ahead of Labour. Certainly, on the basis of by-election performances since mid-1986, the Alliance seemed once again on an upswing.

The overall electoral position, however, was not especially favourable. Some of the best by-election successes had been

Table 3   *Alliance by-election performance, July 1985–March 1987*

Date	Constituency	%change in Lib/SDP vote
4.7.85	Brecon and Radnor	+11.4
6.12.85	Tyne Bridge	+11.4
10.4.86	Fulham	+ 0.6
8.5.86	Ryedale	+19.8
8.5.86	Derbyshire West	+12.3
17.7.86	Newcastle-under-Lyme	+17.7
13.11.86	Knowsley North	+19.8
26.2.87	Greenwich	+27.8
12.3.87	Truro	+ 3.1

secured against the Conservatives, but the Conservative lead in the polls seemed secure when it came to the question of choosing the next government. The recession of the early 1980s was now well past, the economy was moving ahead rapidly and both inflation and unemployment were falling. Council house sales and the first privatizations appeared successful policies with the electorate. Although Labour's new leader, Neil Kinnock, was pursuing a campaign to modernize the organization and image of the Party, he was still burdened with much of the policy incubus which had dragged Labour to defeat in 1983 and remained stubbornly unpopular with the electorate. The municipal elections of May 1987 produced encouraging signs for the Conservatives. While the Alliance made a good showing, gaining 400 seats, there was no dramatic breakthrough, giving the Conservatives sufficient confidence to call an election in June 1987.

The Alliance campaigned on a manifesto *Britain United: The Time has Come*. The situation which had beset the 1983 campaign when Jenkins had been described as 'Prime Minister designate' was replaced by a joint leadership of the campaign by David Owen and David Steel. The Alliance sought, if it held the balance of power, to curb the excesses of both main parties and to initiate its 'Great Reform Charter', proposing electoral reform, repeal of the Official Secrets Act, a Freedom of Information Act, regional government and fixed-term parliaments. The offer to work with other parties attracted inevitable media attention, but it was not always clear that the two Alliance leaders were themselves in agreement about which party was the partner of preference. It was a difficult question for the Alliance to answer in any case – judging 'the issues on their merits' sounded vague and inconclusive, but with two leaders the credibility gap seemed even wider. In a critical interview of both leaders on the BBC's *Panorama* during the campaign, David Owen seemed to indicate that he regarded the Conservatives as more likely partners because of his own views on multilateralism and his distrust of Labour on the issue. Many regarded this as a dangerous breech in the carefully contrived position of not stating in advance of the election a preference for either party.

The following day *The Times* spoke of division between the two Alliance leaders. More worrying, it made it difficult for Alliance candidates to capitalize as effectively as they might have on the anti-Conservative vote. The two factors, apparent disunity and an equally apparent preference on the part of one of the Alliance leaders for Conservatives, damaged the prospects for an advance on the position in 1983. A third factor, too, came into play. The increasingly presidential nature of the election campaign was not conducive to the success of the two-leader experiment by the Alliance. The Conservative campaign was built around Mrs Thatcher as one of the most determined of Britain's post-war leaders. Her role in the Falklands conflict, her brave showing after the Brighton hotel bombing, her rapport with world leaders such as Reagan and the new Soviet leader Gorbachev and her tough stance against the trade unions, notably in the miners' strike of 1984–5, made her style and quality of leadership a major, if not *the* major, issue of the election. Labour responded by presenting Neil Kinnock in similarly presidential terms with slick party political broadcasts and well-managed rallies. In contrast, the Alliance's joint leadership and the open question and answer sessions conducted by both Alliance leaders up and down the country failed to make a distinctive impact. The result of the 1987 election was another disappointment. With 22.7 per cent of the vote the Alliance obtained only 22 seats. The Conservatives, staying ahead in the polls almost throughout the campaign, scored another smashing victory by almost a hundred seats. Labour, though fighting what many saw as an excellent campaign, had secured just over 30 per cent of the vote, not sufficient to trouble the Conservatives but enough to win 229 seats.

The results of the second general election since the formation of the SDP and the conclusion of the Alliance with the Liberals seemed to many to be a good moment for taking stock. It was evident that the Alliance had failed to break the mould of British politics in so far as it had not replaced either of the other two major parties. Most obviously, the Labour Party under its vigorous new leader was in no mood to give up the fight, nor was it damaged irreparably. Even with a depressed share of the vote, there was little likelihood of the Labour Party having less than 150-200 seats in the Commons simply because of the way the electoral geography of the country operated. Although there was convincing evidence that a degree of electoral dealignment was taking place, sufficient to give the Alliance one vote in four, the concentration of Labour's vote gave the Party a durability which had too easily been overlooked in the throes of Labour's civil war after 1979. It would have required a much deeper schism in the Party and its supporters to supplant Labour. Moreover, the very qualities of the traditional Labour Party which so antago-nized its critics, its close ties with the unions and the innate conservatism of much of its support, also gave it a strength to survive in adversity. As an established party still commanding vastly greater resources than the Alliance as well as the loyalty and adherence of millions of voters, it remained obstinately in place as the major opposition party. There could be little doubt, too, that the process of modernization and revamping begun by Kinnock could go still further. Policy had remained Labour's Achilles heel, particularly on defence, Europe and economic policy: with little effective criticism of Kinnock's conduct of the election he was likely to be given the opporutnity to attend to the major weaknesses in Labour's position.

The third-party battleground

Impartial observers noted that British electoral politics in the 1980s had reverted to a situation not dissimilar to the 1930s: if not a three-party situation, then at least a 'two-and-a-half-party' situation, whose electoral consequences proved entirely bene-ficial to the Conservatives. In both 1983 and 1987, the Conser-vatives had gained thumping majorities with just under 43 per cent of the votes cast. A divided opposition had twice allowed the Conservatives to maximize their majority with a share of the vote which had often consigned parties to opposition status between 1945 and 1979. Given the disposition of electoral support, the Conservatives were not likely to face serious consequences until the Alliance vote was raised substantially and Labour also improved its performance. Most critical of all was the vast tract of Southern and suburban England where the Alliance polled respectably but not well enough to threaten a large number of Conservative seats. Moreover, the much-publicized issue of 'tactical voting' where anti-Conservative voters made a rational decision to support whichever party had the best chance of unseating the Tories had some effect in building up support behind the most prominent opposition party, but it had not proved decisive in more than a few seats. Unless it was adopted on a more widespread and consistent basis it was impossible for the opposition parties to maximize their potential number of seats. With a pact between the Alliance and the Labour Party often raised as press speculation but never a likely prospect, the Government enjoyed most of the fruits of a divided opposition.

In effect, Britain consisted of two or even three different electoral battlegrounds in the 1980s. There was a large part of Southern Britain which, if one excluded Greater London, was virtually devoid of Labour MPs. The residual effect of Labour's period of office in 1974–9 and its move to the left in 1979–83, combined with Mrs Thatcher's successful appeal to the new owner-occupiers and taxpayers, meant that Labour after 1983 held only two seats in Southern England outside Greater London. For those with a long memory, it was a position which had a remarkable parallel in the situation after the 1935 election, when Labour was still recovering from the débâcle of the 1931 crisis and had yet to make the huge inroads into 'middle-England' which brought it victory in 1945. In a sense, Labour's tide of support as a party of the middle and more prosperous working class seemed to have been rolled back. The result was that in scores of the constituencies in the South, the Alliance was the second party, but one still too weak to reap more than a handful of seats. North of a line between the Severn and the Wash remained much of the Labour heartland, the old industrial areas. The Alliance had hoped, even more than the Liberal Party in the past, to present themselves as an attractive alternative to the Labour Party in industrial Britain. In practice, however, apart from a scattering of seats and by-election successes, the Alliance had conspicuously failed to break Labour's dominant position in the industrial areas. The spectacular by-election gains, Crosby, Ryedale, Brecon and Radnor, had usually either been suburban seats or ones with a mixed rural-urban electrorate. The Alliance gain in 1987 at Southport was hardly typical of much of the solid Labour territory that the Alliance had set out to win at its inception. The snag was that the Alliance could occasionally do well enough to keep hopes alive that this breakthrough might still happen, particularly if Labour fell into terminal disarray. Warrington, the harbinger of the Alliance, had been just the sort of seat the SDP saw itself as having been formed to win; the by-elections at Tyne Bridge in 1985 and Newcastle-under-Lyme in 1986 had not been too discouraging; and Rochdale and Colne Valley were evidence that the Alliance could win in largely working-class Northern seats. The odds, however, remained more highly stacked against the Alliance in the industrial areas as long as Labour remained an unbroken power. The major confrontation in these areas remained between Labour and the Conservatives; the Tory marginals of the North-West and West Midlands two of the crucial electoral battlegrounds between them and Labour. The relatively marginal impact of the Alliance upon this contest was revealed after the 1987 election when a list of the 29 seats where the Alliance had come closest to winning showed a heavy predominance of rural and suburban seats, 19 of which lay in the South and South-West of the country.

A third electoral pattern could be discerned in Scotland. There the situation was different from the rest of Britain in two important respects. First, the presence of the Scottish Nationalists provided a force which could rival the Liberals as an alternative to the two major parties. But, second, Scotland displayed a marked swing against the Conservatives in the 1980s, leaving Labour in the dominant position enjoyed by Conservatives south of the border. For the former, the existence of a full slate of SNP candidates from the 1970s rivalled Alliance pretensions to be the exclusive third force. However, with the majority of Scottish seats still taken either by Labour or the Conservatives, the 'main game' was between the major parties. Its main feature – in contrast to the rest of Britain – was the failure of the Conservatives, pinned back to a mere seven Scottish seats after the 1987 election, making Scotland a major success story for Labour in an otherwise wretched decade. Increasingly, there was talk of a special 'Scotland effect' in reaction to Mrs Thatcher, in which Scots seemed prepared to vote for whichever party had the best chance of unseating the Tories. Although the principal beneficiary was Labour, the SNP remained a powerful contestant. Its share of the vote, while lower than in 1974, remained sufficient to win it parity of Scottish seats with the Alliance in general elections and to offer a challenge at by-elections. Although severely dented by the devolution débâcle and subsequent factionalism, by 1987 the SNP was effectively back in the fight in Scottish politics and jostling with both the Conservatives and the Alliance for the non-Labour vote. From the Alliance point of view, Scotland was another area where they had failed to make a decisive break-through, faced with a powerful Labour upsurge and the added competition of the SNP.

Table 4   *The SNP 1970–1987*

Election	Candidates	MPs elected	% of Scottish vote
1970	65	1	11.4
1974 (Feb)	70	7	21.9
1974 (Oct)	71	11	30.4
1979	71	2	17.3
1983	71	2	11.8
1987	71	3	14.0

Faced with the electoral reality of only 22 MPs after six years of the Alliance and the fading of all the high hopes of breaking the mould, everything pointed to the need to reappraise the whole future and nature of the Alliance. It was a reappraisal which was to bring about its end and the acrimonious birth of a newly-fashioned third force, the Social and Liberal Democrats.

The Alliance balance sheet

Why the Alliance failed to break the mould has several different explanations. First, there was the way in which the electoral system worked to disadvantage a third force. Although from the 1960s it became evident that the two-party duopoly of British politics was being modified, the two major parties remained dominant in the 1980s in terms of seats won. Even in the Alliance's best election, 1983, Labour and the Conservatives still managed to take 70 per cent of the total vote. This continued dominance was translated into an even higher percentage of the total number of seats by two subsidiary factors: the operation of the first-past-the-post system and the relatively even spread of Alliance support across the country. The effect of these two factors in combination was to give the two main parties a much higher percentage of the total number of seats than their percentage of the total vote. The Conservative vote would have had to fall significantly below the levels it reached in 1983 and 1987 to lose large numbers of seats. Labour would have had to lose support even more substantially before its haul of seats was eroded in large numbers. As one calculation pointed out, even on 20 per cent of the vote, Labour would still have 150 seats because of the concentration of its support.

By both historical and contemporary analogies, the Alliance was peculiarly disadvantaged during the 1980s. As Chris Cook has pointed out, 23 per cent of the vote had brought the Liberal Party 59 seats in 1929 when the traditional Liberal vote was still to some extent concentrated; in 1923 it had obtained 158 seats with a vote of 29 per cent. In that sense, the Alliance suffered from the same problem as the Liberals in the past, only more so. It could pile up a large popular vote but still find itself denied more than a small percentage of seats. Thus, although the Alliance in 1983 was able to raise the third-party vote six percentage points higher than the best result achieved by the Liberals alone since 1945, in February 1974, it brought only marginally more seats and failed to dislodge substantially the

Table 5 *Party share of votes and seats 1970–1992*

Year	Con and Lab combined		All other parties		Liberals (Alliance, 1983 and 1987)	
	% of vote	% of seats	% of vote	% of seats	% of vote	% of seats
1970	89.4	98.1	10.6	1.9	7.5	0.95
1974 (Feb)	74.9	94.2	25.1	5.8	19.3	2.21
1974 (Oct)	75.0	93.9	25.0	6.1	18.3	2.05
1979	80.9	95.6	19.1	4.4	13.8	1.73
1983	70.0	92.0	30.0	8.0	25.4	3.54
1987	73.1	91.8	26.9	8.2	22.6	3.38

two-party dominance of seats. In contrast, a regionally based party like the SNP, could obtain 11 seats at Westminster with a mere 2.9 per cent of the vote in October 1974, half the seats the Alliance obtained in 1987 with eight times the number of votes. Hypothetically, the Alliance would have done better if its support had been more concentrated, for example on the traditional areas of Liberal support or, in the case of the SDP, in metropolitan, Southern England where its appeal was strongest. In fact, in the two elections the Alliance fought, the Liberals were the more successful Alliance partner because their candidates were fighting more seats where they had built up a base of support. The SDP found themselves, in contrast, defending seats won with earlier party labels or by-election victories, often with only a thin layer of support and organization. As a result, both general and municipal elections in the 1980s tended to see the Liberals emerge as the more successful Alliance partner in electoral terms. From their dominant position in the Alliance shortly after its formation, the SDP was reduced to six MPs in 1983 and to five in 1987. Similarly, while the Liberals were able to make three gains in 1987, the SDP failed to gain any and only David Owen of the original 'Gang of Four' remained in the Commons.

But the second feature which underlay this situation was the resilience of the two main parties as political entities. The Conservatives were able to rebound from periods of deep unpopularity in 1981–2 and 1985–6 to win major victories. Although the size of its majorities were to a large extent artificially inflated by the divisions of the opposition parties, its ability to win over 40 per cent of the vote in the two general elections of the 1980s illustrated that it was *the* party the others had to beat if they were to have a hope of putting their policies into practice. Apart from Scotland, there was little evidence that the Conservatives were a dwindling force. Although losing control of local government in a large number of urban areas to either Labour, Alliance or 'hung' councils, the Conservative's ability to fight their way out of electoral troughs and regain the initiative in time for general election campaigns showed them to be a powerful and effective political force which neither of the opposition parties had been able to weaken seriously. Labour, too, in spite of its turmoil in the early 1980s, survived aided by its concentrated electoral base, union support and the adherence of all those who did *not* join the SDP breakaway. After 1983 there was a distinct revival in Labour fortunes under the new leadership of Kinnock. While Labour's electoral performance was depressed, it was not depressed enough to bring about the Party's disintegration. By 1987 the creation of the SDP looked more like a schismatic breakaway than a fatal rupture. There was no evidence that the Labour Party was going to disappear, even if there remained doubts about its ability ever to win a parliamentary majority on its own again.

Third, the Alliance could be said to have failed to maximize its own appeal by not moving quickly enough to merge the two constituent parties and make a more effective challenge. The failure to merge the parties cost support in various ways. The inevitable squabbles and rivalries of any two groups working together diverted energies and attracted adverse publicity. To the chagrin of the Alliance, high-minded and genuine attempts to make a virtue of co-operation between two parties was outweighed by the poor publicity that differences over policy and tactics attracted. Merger would not necessarily have resolved these problems or the habitual tendency of the media to personalize and factionalize political debate within political parties. After all, both Labour and the Conservatives were for much of the decade dogged by encapsulations of their own divisions in terms of left and right and 'wets' and 'dries'. But acute self-consciousness about the press and media response to early arguments over seat allocation and, later, over policy towards nuclear weapons, reflected the degree to which the Alliance was dependent on favourable media coverage to expand its base of support. The initial launch of the SDP had been boosted precisely because it was a major media event – the formation of a new party. As the Alliance struggled to get onto level terms with the other parties while at the same time portraying itself as a more principled and high-minded alternative, it proved vulnerable to anything which tarnished its clean, rational image. Once the initial euphoria of the Alliance was spent and it bedded down as an electoral force, the main effect of having two parties working together was to confuse its appeal to the electrorate. Lack of distinctiveness – the old Liberal bugbear – was now compounded by having two parties and, after 1983, two leaders.

The failure to merge the two parties was an undoubted handicap by 1987. Although the Alliance name had become well-recognized, it was too easy for both opponents and the media to seek out differences between the leaders and the parties. But the difficulty with merging lay in the fact that there were two diffrent tendencies represented in the formation of the SDP. One, most strongly represented by Roy Jenkins, saw the SDP as the first step along the road to realignment in British politics, with the merger of the Liberals and the SDP following fairly quickly on the Alliance. Crudely, the SDP was a means rather than an end in itself: the means whereby support which had not yet joined the Liberals could be brought into politics and a half-way house for those wishing to leave the Labour and Conservative parties but who were not yet ready to align themselves directly with the Liberals. Others, however, of whom David Owen, John Cartwright and Rosie Barnes proved the most conspicuous, saw the SDP as having an identity of its own. For them the SDP was a new party, one which allowed a group largely composed of Labour moderates to fashion the kind of social democratic party they believed had evolved elsewhere in Europe and which had been frustrated by the old-style Labour Party. For these people, the SDP was an end in itself; they jealously guarded their distinctive policy positions and their purpose-built democratic constitutional structure, and saw the Alliance as about as far as they were prepared to go along the road of losing their identity as a separate party. To that extent the SDP was almost too successful in establishing itself for merger to become an immediate possibility. The Alliance was forced to retain a split political personality.

Fourth, the Alliance also carried over another legacy of the Liberals which was the dilemma of exactly where it stood in the political spectrum and what kind of appeal it was making to the electorate. To an extent it was an inevitable confusion: whether the Alliance stood for a left-of-centre platform trying to replace the Labour Party or was a centre party trying to draw support from both left and right, from the moderate middle-ground. Initially, the SDP's stated position was quite clear, that it was a genuine party of social democracy which was attempting to break free of the 'loony left' which had come to dominate the Labour party of Michael Foot and the institutional brake upon the development of Labour caused by its close association with the trade unions. It was often forgotten that the occasion for the formation of the Council of Social Democracy was the special Wembley Conference vote in 1981 which gave the trade unions a major say in who should become Labour leader. Multilateralism, support for Nato and for the Common Market were also defining characteristics, as was a rejection of the old-style nationalization and corporatism which still formed central features of Labour Party policy as late as 1983. But the SDP was always a little more than revamped Gaitskellism. Its democratic structure and policy-making procedures and its challenge to the existing political framework in attempting to promote electoral reform and freedom of information also gave it a genuinely radical edge. The difficulty was that many Liberals suspected the SDP's radical credentials. To them David Owen seemed more interested in preserving an independent nuclear deterrent and the 'social market' than in proportional representation or regional government. Ageing 'Young Liberals' and the Liberal activists strongly represented in the former Association of Liberal Councillors feared being dragged along in the wake of a centralized and centrist leadership. Years of grass roots campaigning and community politics had made distrust of their own leadership, especially after the Lib-Lab pact, and almost anything emanating from London one of the motifs of Liberal Party politics. The close partnership which David Steel strove to build with David Owen was bound to create tensions and the nuclear issue was the one on which the radical wing of the Liberals chose to make its views felt.

The row over nuclear weapons in the autumn of 1986 was a symptom of tensions and confusions over policy which ran through other areas of debate, particularly as under Owen's leadership the SDP began to espouse what was known as the 'social market' philosophy. Although this was rejected by the Council, the supreme policy-making body of the SDP, in 1987, it reinforced an impression combined with Dr Owen's strong views on defence policy, that the SDP was moving more to the right. This apparent drift in the policy spectrum, radical on constitutional matters, managerial and interventionist in the economic sphere and hawkish on defence, produced confusion or at least a lack of clear identity. 'What does the Alliance stand for?' was the question which most of its canvassers and candidates were still being asked in 1987 as much as in 1981. The paradox was that the Alliance was positively overloaded with policy. Liberal Assemblies, the Association of Alliance Councillors and the various groups within the Liberal Party were no less ready to formulate policy on almost every conceivable issue as they had been in the 1970s. The SDP came onto the political scene not only with a group of experienced politicians with their own political agenda, but also quickly recruited heavily from academics and professionals who began work on policy documents. In January 1982, the SDP launched the 'Tawney Society' in self-conscious rivalry to the Fabian Society and the Conservative 'think-tanks' to stimulate policy discussion.

Public perception, however, was not clarified by the range of issues and wealth of detail which became a hallmark of Alliance policy-making. It was not helped by the position the Alliance was in tactically, which helped to confuse its image between a radical and a centrist stance. The SDP had set out to replace the Labour Party as the principal party of opposition, placing it somewhere on the left of the political spectrum, but the evident failure to dislodge the Labour Party from its place as the official opposition in the House of Commons forced the Alliance increasingly to talk the language of 'holding the balance'. By 1987 there was little doubt that the most realistic aim of the Alliance *was* to hold the balance of power in a hung Parliament. This view was reinforced by claims expressed from an early stage that the Alliance sought to curb the 'excesses' of the other parties and by the role of Alliance groups where they controlled or held the balance in hung councils up and down the country. It was not difficult for the electorate to conclude that the Alliance, like the Liberals before them, were some kind of centre party. However genuine the protestations the Alliance might make about being a radical party of reform, their electoral position made a different view by the electorate almost inevitable.

Fifth, as is often the case, what does not happen in politics is as important as what does. In the 1970s the Liberals had two opportunities to prop up minority governments, one of which they had taken in the Lib-Lab pact. But the effect of three decisive Conservative majorities in the 1979, 1983 and 1987 General Elections was to deny the Liberals and then the Alliance any share of effective power. The backstairs route to influence on government under what was seen as an electoral system peculiarly disadvantageous to the Alliance and its large popular vote was denied them. But while the electoral system remained unreformed it was the most likely prospect of obtaining major influence or even a share of government. The possibility of having sufficient MPs to hold the balance of power was, in fact, to remain the best hope of playing a significant role in politics for a third party like the Alliance. It was an opportunity which Mrs Thatcher's crushing victories was to deny them. This also bore upon another part of the realignment of British politics which came to nothing. Although attention was concentrated upon the travails of Labour in the early 1980s, Liberals in the 1970s had put out some feelers to Liberal Tories. It was not totally unrealistic to suppose that some of the 'wetter' Tories might have joined the breakaway from Labour. One did, but no one else followed. The refusal of any substantial portion of the Tory Party to break away from the Thatcher Government prevented, as much as the limited schism in Labour, the Alliance having a large enough bloc of support to alter the balance of power in the Commons. With a post-1979 Conservative majority of under 50 seats, the failure of the Tory 'wets' to join the realignment offered by the Alliance was one of the most significant aspects of its failure.

What, if anything, had the Alliance achieved? First, the accession of the SDP leadership had given a whole new dimension to the credibility of a third force in British politics. Taken together, the Liberals and SDP looked like an alternative government in the way the Liberals had not on their own. *The Economist* was only slightly mocking when in December 1981 it carried a picture of David Steel, Shirley Williams and Roy Jenkins on its cover with the headline 'Her Majesty's new opposition' – there was not even a question mark. The early days of the Alliance were then an enormous boost for the credibility of an alternative to the two main parties and indeed raised the possibility that one of them might be replaced.

But, second, even when that did not happen, and the euphoria of the early Alliance was spent, it had brought three-party politics into operation for the first time for more than 50 years. In the polls, in the media and in elections, the Alliance seemed finally to have put paid to a return to a two-party system. The Alliance ratchetted up support for a third force to a new peak. Although this was to lead to an equally dizzying decline at the time of the merger negotiations and mass defections in poll support, once the new, merged party established itself it was able to resume the role of an alternative home for political support to the two other parties.

Third, the Alliance vote in 1983 and 1987 and the survival of a viable third party commanding significant poll support and capable of winning major by-election victories raised the spectre that Labour might not be capable of winning power on its own again. The 'knock-on' effects on Labour were important, spurring on its policy review and a revamping of its image. By the early 1990s, it was not inconceivable that Labour would 'convert' to proportional representation. This was a fourth effect, in that the Alliance had helped to put the question of proportional representation higher up the public agenda. A largely dead issue with the electorate in 1979, the endorsement by the SDP leaders of the need for major constitutional reform, including a fairer voting system, raised the profile of the issue. The Alliance's performance became self-educational not only for its activists but also for a wider public as a party attracting a large share of the vote but denied a proportionate share of seats both in local and parliamentary elections.

Fifth, it was easy to fail to recognize amidst the drama and personalities of the Alliance years a simple fact. What had begun with the creation of a new party, the SDP, had ended with a merger with the older third force, the Liberals. For some SDP die-hards, it was not difficult to argue that the Liberals had hijacked their party, not so much strangled it at birth, but smothered and finally absorbed it. This ignored the extent to which the Liberals felt they had made genuine sacrifices, especially in the 1983 election, to accommodate SDP candidates; the real extent of co-operation on the ground which had made merger almost a foregone conclusion by 1987, especially in local government and in individual constituencies; and the extent to which the merged party which resulted drew heavily on former SDP policy and practice, for example over membership and constitution. The Alliance years had not just been the latest and largest Liberal revival. However, there were cumulative effects which had something of that character, for, finally, the Alliance had built upon the support in local government won by the Liberals. The advent of the SDP brought an influx of new activists and prospective candidates for local government. Although the fortunes of the Alliance in the annual May council elections were to some extent dictated by the factors which influenced parliamentary general elections and by-elections, the system of rotating elections with only a proportion of seats being contested each year allowed some smoothing out of the rapid fluctuations in Alliance support. By the mid-eighties the Alliance had over 3,000 councillors and had control or decisive influence in a number of different councils up and down the country. As the number of Alliance councillors grew, the most typical situation was to create situations of no overall control. Even with the failures of the parliamentary group to expand more rapidly, the Alliance had become an established presence in local government even if it still represented a smaller corpus of candidates than either of the main parties. In a sense, the Alliance's local base remained the part of the iceberg invisible beneath the surface. It was to form a crucial ingredient in the survival of a third force when the process of reappraisal after the 1987 election turned into a protracted and bitter merger.

6 A New Third Force: The Social and Liberal Democrats, 1988–1992

The 1987 election result was especially disappointing for the Alliance. The Conservatives could congratulate themselves on a stunning triumph which gave Mrs Thatcher a hatrick of victories – the first Prime Minister since Lord Liverpool to win three successive election victories. The defeated Labour Party had run a professional and well-managed campaign which, while not noticeably raising the Labour vote during the election, created a favourable, more modern image. Above all, it had raised its vote since 1983 and moved more decisively ahead of the Alliance. For the Alliance itself, there was a distinct sense of impasse. Far from breaking the mould, its overall vote had fallen by over 400,000 and its share of the poll by almost three percentage points. The number of MPs returned was one less than in 1983 and there was a net loss of five seats compared with the Alliance's strength in the Commons at the time of the dissolution.

'Democratic fusion'

The need to rethink the Alliance's position was pressing. Reappraisal, however, was precipitated more quickly than almost anyone expected by David Steel's call for a 'democratic fusion' of the two wings of the Alliance on the weekend following the general election. David Owen's no less swift declaration against merger and call for a ballot of the SDP membership brought the long-simmering issue of whether to merge the two parties to a head. Grass-roots parties were already beginning to fuse and in spite of fierce resistance from Owen and some other SDP members against attempts to 'bounce' them into a merger, a ballot on opening talks with the Liberals was agreed on 29 June. On 6 August the ballot showed a majority of 57.4 per cent in favour of merger discussions. Owen promptly resigned as leader, leaving the almost unknown Robert MacLennan as caretaker leader of the SDP. It was immediately apparent that the SDP was split into two camps and that a section of SDP members, led by Owen, were against any merger with the Liberals.

The merger talks proved lengthy and difficult. Instead of a swift and revitalizing 'fusion' of the two parties, the negotiations dragged on into the winter of 1987–8 with growing demoralization and evident loss of support. The sudden loss of David Owen and his clear determination to resist all overtures to join any merged body, cast a pall over the merger process: 'fusion' began to look suspiciously like disarray. None the less, those committed to the merger process battled on. Problems about the name of the new body and its draft statement of principles caused high drama during the first part of 1988, but by late January there was something to ratify. At a special conference in Blackpool in January, the Liberal Party overwhelmingly endorsed the merger and, with it, the end of the old Liberal Party in adopting a new name, the Social and Liberal Democrats. On 31 January, the Council of the SDP meeting at Sheffield also voted by a large majority in favour of the new party. This result, however, was somewhat upstaged by David Owen using the Council venue to hold a rally for a 'continuing SDP'. Almost at the moment of climax for the protracted merger process, clear disunity in the old Alliance was made public by the extensive media coverage for Owen and the supporting MPs in his stand on the SDP's survival, John Cartwright and Rosie Barnes. The Liberals, too, suffered their body of dissenters. Though less significant numerically or in personalities, a group of 'independent Liberals', bent on retaining the old party name and with a base of support in Michael Meadowcroft's constituency in West Yorkshire, seemed to create yet more splinters of the old Alliance. With the formal approval of the merger in a ballot of the SDP membership declared on 2 March, the final obstacle to the launch of the Social and Liberal Democrats, on 3 March, was overcome. The SDP ballot, however, while showing a comfortable majority for merger (65.3 per cent) also revealed a substantial minority, greater than in the SDP Council, against. It was clear that there was a sizeable constituency among former SDP members for retaining a distinct party. On 8 March what had threatened took effect when Owen relaunched the SDP and was elected leader with John Cartwright as President.

The period between the June 1987 General Election and March 1988 had seen a bewildering series of events for third-party politics. David Steel's attempt to bring about the merger he had long aimed for had been far more protracted and acrimonious than anyone had expected. Few had anticipated the determination of three of the five SDP MPs and especially Owen to resist the wishes of the majority of their Party for merger. The reasons, if one discounted suggestions of mere personal ambition, lay in the original split personality of the SDP between those who had always seen the future in terms of a merged party and those who stressed the SDP's unique identity. That this was a genuine split was shown by the way the Parliamentary Party divided, two MPs for merger, three against. The SDP in the Lords also contained a group who wished to retain their indepedent identity, as did a group of articulate supporters in the country. To infuriated Liberals and pro-merger SDPers it was difficulty to understand how Owen and his followers could defy a majority decision in a party which had founded itself on democratic principles. The charge of egoism and not being a 'team player' were easy enough to lay at Owen's door; he could, however, claim a consistent adherence to a separate SDP and having not shared the view of the other members of the 'Gang of Four' that merger was the SDP's inevitable destiny.

Third-party disarray

The Social and Liberal Democrats were therefore launched in the worst possible circumstances. The SLD and the continuing SDP were now rivals for the old Alliance vote. Not surprisingly, the nine months since June 1987 had seen a huge loss of support in the polls and a steady loss of members and activists. The SLD and the SDP seemed intent on destroying each other, not only splitting the former Alliance share but also reducing their combined support as a credible alternative to Labour and the Conservatives. Under the temporary joint leadership of David Steel and Andrew MacLennan the new Party quickly faced two tests. The first was the local elections of May 1988. As anticipated, the new SLD lost ground, with a net loss of over 60 council seats; but taken over the broad spectrum of seats being defended, the losses were fairly marginal and the party had secured a vote considerably better that its current opinion poll ratings. More encouragingly, the weakness of the continuing SDP was ruthlessly exposed, defending only a fraction of the seats of the SLD and losing heavily. The second test was the question of leadership, held in abeyance until after the local elections had been fought. Following the local elections, as widely anticipated, David Steel declared that he would not be a candidate for the leadership. By the opening of the eight-week election campaign in June 1988, the two candidates were Paddy Ashdown and Alan Beith. In a series of 'hustings meetings' up and down the country, it soon became apparent that there were few differences of principle between the candidates: more ones of personality and strategy. Ashdown's insistence that the SLD must replace the Labour Party was met by Beith's argument that such a strategy was unrealistic. The outcome, however, was a decisive victory for Ashdown by a large majority.

UNIVERSITY OF
WOLVERHAMPTON
DUDLEY CAMPUS LIBRARY

Ashdown had an unusual background to stand in succession to the past leaders of the Liberal Party and of the Alliance. A former marine commando and executive, he was seen as an attractive, fresh personality who had built up a winning position in his own constituency of Yeovil as a Liberal from third place by almost classic community campaigning. But as an MP of only five years' standing, he was bound to face difficulties as a largely unknown quantity to the electorate in establishing himself as a credible leader of an effective third force.

Meanwhile the opinion polls were registering a major loss of public support for both the old Alliance partners, putting them at less than half of their rating in the general election 12 months earlier. While the leadership contest was under way the SLD and continuing SDP faced their first parliamentary by-election at Kensington. Neither emerged very creditably: the SLD was unable to repeat anything like the spectacular bandwagon effect of earlier by-elections, its only crumb of comfort being that the SDP candidate obtained fewer votes and almost lost his deposit.

The first conferences since the break-up of the Alliance were eagerly awaited to see how the ex-partners would fare. The SDP's conference at Torquay (September 1988) was notable for David Owen's clear declaration that his party would continue and his espousal of the issue of electoral reform as a main plank in the SDP's programme. The SLD conference at Blackpool (September 1988) was immediately pitched into a passionate debate about the short name by which the party would be known. To the evident dismay of some ex-Liberals, a clear majority accepted the title of Democrats. With by- and Euro-elections pending, however, the future of the old Alliance partners still appeared to hang in the balance. The Richmond and Epping Forest by-elections seemed to show that the existence of two parties claiming to stand for an alternative to Labour and the Conservatives was likely to diffuse any possible third-party breakthrough. A good second place at Epping by the Social and Liberal Democrats might have been a victory in other circumstances. At Richmond, the SDP was able to take second place over the SLD, exposing how effectively their rivalry could spoil any advance by the Democrats as well as denying either party a by-election success.

The situation was so serious that Ashdown offered an electoral truce to the SDP after the Richmond by-election. But, in practice, it was easier for the SDP to put up candidates for occasional by-elections and register a significant showing in the nationally-conducted opinion polls than to maintain the pretensions of a fully-fledged party. Its local base was extremely small, the great majority of former Alliance councillors and activists having joined the merged party. The Social and Liberal Democrats were, in fact, stronger than their poll ratings and parliamentary by-election results showed. In the 1988 local elections the SLD had put forward over 1,700 candidates, the SDP only 280. The SLD had 303 elected, the SDP only 4. In local by-elections from March 1988 to March 1989, the SLD had elected 87 councillors against the SDP's single success. The SLD share of the vote was also much higher than its poll ratings suggested, at an average of 30.8 per cent in seats contested over the 12 months up to March 1989. It was the local strength of the SLD, building on the earlier success of the Liberals and the Alliance, which gave the SLD some resilience during its most difficult period. The May 1989 local elections saw this disparity between the former Alliance partners confirmed. The SLD was defending 619 seats compared with the SDP's 31. In the past 12 months the SLD had little difficulty in obtaining candidates, contesting 307 of 394 by-elections since March 1988, while the SDP could find only 47. By April 1989, the SLD had been able to put up 2,254 candidates for the 3,565 seats available. Although the May local elections saw the SLD lose seats, more than a hundred, this was less than had been feared, well down on the 200 expected losses Ashdown had been suggesting as late as January. Although the opinion polls were showing support in single figures, the average share of the poll in the May elections was 20 per cent. There was considerable variation in the success rate over the country, but SLD support seemed to be holding up especially well in areas where the Liberals had built up a strong position before and during the Alliance.

The challenge of the Greens

The next test of strength came a month later in the Euro-elections of June 1989. The initial background to the elections seemed promising. The Owenite SDP had decided to withdraw as a national force following its evident inability to contest effectively anything like a full slate of local council seats. But the SLD was faced with serious financial problems and what amounted to something close to organizational fatigue. It was decided not to put much central effort into the Euro-elections, leaving it to local parties to find the substantial deposits required for Euro-constituencies and meet the cost of the campaign themselves. At a critical juncture in the life of the new party this was an understandable decision. Unfortunately, it occurred just at the point when a new force was appearing on the scene. The sudden revival of environmental concern in 1988–9 brought about by new evidence about global warming and damage to the ozone layer gave an enormous boost to the Green Party. From a minor force as fringe candidates in local elections, their support mushroomed to fill the vacuum left by the disarray in the old Alliance partners. It was the Greens who were to demonstrate just how much damage the merger had done to the Social and Liberal Democrats. In the June Euro-elections they found themselves beaten into fourth place in the overall vote by the Greens. The SLD received only 6 per cent of votes cast while the Greens scored almost 15 per cent.

Suddenly, all the media attention previously concentrated on the Alliance and its doings switched to the new phenomenon. The new party attracted a flood of new members, some at least of them ex-Liberals disillusioned by the more professional ethos which Ashdown was attempting to breathe into his struggling party. The national opinion polls showed the Greens ahead of the SLD, now well down in single figures. As well as losing support the SLD's financial difficulties were so serious that much of the headquarters staff had to be sacked and the network of regional agents disbanded. Membership had fallen to about 75,000, 5,000 less than those who had voted in the leadership contest in 1988.

But the local election results proved a more reliable guide than the Euro-elections to the fate of the SLD as the major third party. The SDP was now clearly in decline. Although its sitting MPs remained determined not to join the merged party, it had effectively quit the scene as a national force. Although its demise was a lingering one eventually, in June 1990, the leadership decided to wind up the SDP as a political party while remaining as a pressure group for social democratic policies. Its MPs continued to sit as 'independent SDP' members in the Commons and the SDP group in the Lords remained in existence. The main asset of the old SDP, however, remained David Owen, still considered by many as one of the ablest figures in the Commons. Rumours of overtures with other parties during 1990 and 1991 came to nothing and in September 1991 Owen declared that he was quitting politics. The Greens, too, proved a less effective force than they had appeared for a few months in 1989. The Greens' refusal to play the conventional party game, using a team of spokespersons rather than having a recognized leader, and their espousal of single-issue politics, meant that political commentators found it difficult to believe that the Greens could ever compete as an effective alternative to the major parties. This appeared to be confirmed as their poll ratings began to fall and they failed to secure any by-election successes.

The Social and Liberal Democrats, like other parties, moved swiftly to prove their 'green' credentials. They were in a particularly strong position to do so, being able to demonstrate that they had taken up environmental issues earlier than anyone else. Ashdown was able to make effective use of evidence that the SLD had put green policies into practice in local government. By 1990 the SDP had been rendered impotent, the Green challenge contained and the independent Liberals confined to a minor role. The SNP was a more serious threat in Scotland where it won an important by-election victory in the Labour stronghold of Glasgow Govan in November 1988. The disarray of the old Alliance saw the SNP moving sharply ahead in the Scottish polls, so much so that one System 3 poll for the *Glasgow Herald* in April 1989 put the SNP at 27 per cent compared with the SLD on 7 per cent. Scotland remained a complex electoral battleground, however, and the SLD played an important part in the calling of a constitutional convention which endorsed the call for a devolved Assembly for Scotland. With a strong presence in Scottish local government, half of its MPs sitting for Scottish seats, and two of its 'near misses' in Scotland, as well as prominent figures such as the former Liberal leader, David Steel, involved in the devolution campaign, the SLD remained keenly involved in the battle for the Scottish vote.

A new revival?

By the September 1990 conference, the SLD was hanging on to its modest share of the poll ratings. These remained, generally, in single figures but they were now usually clear of the Greens and 'others' by a margin of a few percentage points. On the eve of the 1990 conference, Gallup gave the Party a rating of 9.3 per cent. More serious was the still widespread confusion about the identity of the Party, a confusion compounded by the changes in name which the Party had undergone. Apart from being the butt of opponents and commentators alike, there was both dissatisfaction among many members with the label of 'Democrats' as a short name and sheer bewilderment from an electorate who had long since lost track of changing names and initials. Gallup revealed the depths of the credibility gap with which the successors to the Alliance were faced when they found that nearly three-quarters of their respondents in September 1990 either did not know the new Party's name or got it wrong; four-fifths either did not know or had no clear idea of what the Social and Liberal Democrats 'stood for'. Gallup virtually had to discount its usual question about whether people took a favourable or unfavourable view of the Party because two-thirds of people knew so little about it they refused to hazard a guess.

Faced with this depth of public ignorance and confusion about its identity, a major revival in fortunes looked a long way off. An initial step which was, in part, a sop to the old Liberal partners in the Alliance was another name change, adopting the short title 'Liberal Democrats'. Ashdown also set out to fashion a distinct platform for the new Party, for example by using his expertise in Far Eastern affairs to good effect in the debate on the future of Hong Kong, and was the only senior politician to suggest the possibility of admitting as many of the Hong Kong Chinese as might wish to enter Britain. In spite of these attempts to sharpen the Party's image, the real political battle appeared to have reverted to one between Labour and the Conservatives. The policy review conducted by Labour had jettisoned much of the electorally disastrous baggage of the early 1980s and by the summer of 1990 it had taken a commanding lead in the polls. By-election victories and a major Labour success in the Euro-elections raised their poll ratings to well over 40 per cent. However the Liberal Democrats might revive, they would be doing so in a context where the Labour Party had lifted itself out of the doldrums and increasingly looked a credible alternative government.

But in a situation where Labour was clearly once again becoming a 'real opposition', the Liberal Democrats were also able to capitalize on the growing unpopularity of the Conservative Government. During 1990 the Conservatives found themselves presiding over rising inflation and high interest rates, increasingly isolated over Europe and suffering bitter criticism over the introduction of the Poll Tax. The last proved the crucial issue of the year. The unpopularity of the Poll Tax surpassed the Government's worst fears with violent demonstrations as well as large-scale non-payment campaigns in Scotland and some English urban areas. Within weeks of the announcement of its levels the Poll Tax was the single most important factor in the Conservative's popularity for a large proportion of the electorate. The tax was also widely identified with Mrs Thatcher and by the autumn of 1990 her own popularity was plummetting. As a result Mrs Thatcher's likening of the Liberal Democrats at the Conservative Party Conference in October 1990 to the 'dead parrot' of the Monty Python sketch was to return to haunt her. A week later, the Liberal Democrats scored a major victory at the Eastbourne by-election. Caused by the murder of the incumbent Ian Gow by an IRA assassination squad, the by-election took place when the first signs of economic downturn were beginning to be felt in the hitherto booming South. But it was also a seat in which the Liberal Democrats had a sustained record in local government and its candidate, David Bellotti, was well known as a county councillor. Assisted by a poor Tory campaign, the Conservatives crashed to a major defeat. A Conservative majority of over 17,000 was overturned and replaced by a majority of 4,550 for the Liberal Democrats. Suddenly, from a point where they had been written off as serious contenders, the old Libreal stand-by of a by-election victory had put the Liberal Democrats back in the headlines.

The following weeks were dominated by the growing drama in the Conservative Party. Eastbourne had helped to convince a sizeable proportion of the party that Mrs Thatcher's style of leadership and the preservation of the Poll Tax were unlikely to give the Conservatives a realistic prospect of victory at the next election. The resignation of Geoffrey Howe on 1 November and his sensational Commons speech a fortnight later plunged the Conservative Party into a leadership crisis. On 22 November Mrs Thatcher, having failed to win an outright majority over Michael Heseltine on the first ballot of the leadership contest, withdrew from the second round. Out of the three candidates who now put themselves forward, Heseltine, Douglas Hurd and John Major, Major secured a sufficiently convincing majority to secure the leadership without a final ballot. Major's immediate problem was tackling the issue which had contributed so much to Mrs Thatcher's downfall, the Poll Tax. At first, Major havered on the issue, seeking modification of a tax which he, like other senior Tory politicians, had approved and defended. Concentration of attention on the Gulf War and a honeymoon period in which the Conservative poll ratings rose offered some relief from the battering which the Conservative Party had taken in the last months of Thatcher's premiership. A by-election in Ribble Valley in rural north Lancashire in March caused by the elevation of the sitting MP David Waddington to the Lords became, however, virtually a one-seat referendum on the Poll Tax. Ribble Valley was the thirteenth safest Conservative seat in the country with a majority of almost 20,000. It saw the second great victory of the Liberal Democrats since the autumn of 1990 with a shock defeat for the Conservatives. With little base in the local government, the Liberal Democrats had capitalized on massive voter dissatisfaction. It was one of the most dramatic by-election successes not only in terms of the size of the majority overturned but because it, in effect, destroyed the Poll Tax. In the subsequent Budget, the Chancellor increased VAT by 2.5 per cent in order to fund an immediate Poll Tax reduction of £140. The measure had all the signs of panic – millions of newly-printed Poll Tax demands had to be scrapped and every single payment recalculated to take into account the new rebate. Two days later, the Environment Minister, Michael Heseltine, finally announced the end of the Poll Tax. Apart from the Orpington by-election which heralded Macmillan's unprecedented Cabinet reshuffle, no sequence of by-elections had probably had more direct impact on politics than the results of Eastbourne and Ribble Valley. If Eastbourne had put Thatcher's continued premiership directly in question, Ribble Valley had destroyed the most unpopular government measure of recent times.

The Liberal Democrats were now beginning to benefit from the familiar afterglow of by-election success. They entered the local council elections in May 1991 anticipating a modest loss of seats. Because of the operation of the electoral cycle in local government, the Liberal Democrats were defending seats won when the Alliance was in full swing three years earlier. The outcome surpassd all expectations, with widespread gains, over 500, rather than the anticipated losses. As a result of these successes, the Libral Democrats entered the autumn conference season of 1991 once again riding a surge in the polls. Having struggled to reach double figures in 1990, on the eve of the September 1991 Party conference at Bournemouth the Liberal Democrats stood at 19.5 per cent in Gallup, within sight of breaking the psychologically important 20 per cent barrier. The principal cause of this rise lay in a weakening of both Labour and Conservative support. While Labour had managed to reach and maintain a 40 per cent rating in the polls, it had fallen from the peaks achieved in the last months of Mrs Thatcher's premiership. The Conservatives had recovered popularity under Major, but the level of support for both parties permitted the Liberal Democrats to exploit a significant wedge of support. Although polls varied as to how high that level of support was, it represented a remarkable comeback from the situation immediately after the new Party was formed. Poll evidence suggested that increasing numbers of the electorate were now able to distinguish the Party and had some idea of its policies. This was assisted by the demise or arrested development of other competing third forces. The SDP was no more after the summer of 1990, while the surge of support for the Greens had become dissipated. Once again, the heirs of the Liberal Party and the Alliance were in the position of being the only effective third party competing for votes throughout mainland Britain.

From being very much an unknown quantity, Paddy Ashdown had developed into an effective party leader. His personal standing in the polls rose substantially between the autumn of 1990 and that of 1991. Indeed, his popularity was even greater than that of his party. In September 1990 only 30.6 per cent of voters thought he was proving a good leader of his party. By August 1991 his standing had risen to 56.2 per cent, higher than Neil Kinnock's as Labour leader. With three untried and relatively inexperienced party leaders competing for the public's attention, Ashdown was able to make the most of his undoubted qualities of energy and enthusiasm. He was also able to begin to strike a distinctive note for his own vision for the Party. Ashdown had always reiterated the claim, so frequently made by Liberal and Alliance leaders in the past, that the new Party was not a mere centre party but a radical party. As the Party began to formulate its policies for the general election that was due by the summer of 1992, Ashdown sought to give the Liberal Democrats a distinctive radical agenda. Free-market economies were unashamedly espoused in economic documents accepted by the Party conference in September, toughening controls on monopolies, committing the Party to decentralized wage bargaining in the public sector and encouraging wealth creation.

Party spokespersons set out to demonstrate that the Liberal Party had always been in favour of economic liberalism and that its adoption by Mrs Thatcher had been marred by a failure to implement it sufficiently rigorously in the world of business and the newly privatized public monopolies. Government would largely quit the scene of economic regulation by making the Bank of England independent of government control on the pattern of the German Bundesbank and committing Britain to the 'narrow band' of Exchange Rate Mechanism (ERM) membership. These policies were complemented by enthusiastic support for European federalism and Economic and Monetary Union. But the acceptance of free-market disciplines and European Monetary Union were offset by a pledge to raise taxes, if necessary, to fund further educational spending. The Party's green dimension was backed up by a commitment to increase taxes on environmental pollutants, including pertrol, and to encourage alternative energy resources. Euro-federalism was also balanced by a commitment to assemblies for Scotland and Wales and to regional government in England. The Liberal Democrats also emphasized their commitment once again to constitutional reform, to proportional representation, a Freedom of Information Act and fixed-term parliaments.

In significant respects, the Liberal Democrats had not only refurbished their policies, melding some of the traditional Liberal issues with a fresh raft of free-market, pro-European and environmental issues, but also adopted a rather more professional approach to politics. One of the most important inputs of the SDP into the Alliance and later the Liberal Democrats was a more regular and systematic party organization. The Liberal Party had functioned like an extended family, in its time a strength which permitted its survival and allowed it to draw more than usual levels of commitment from many of its members and activists. The Party had inherited a somewhat ramshackle structure in which particular groups and the parties of Wales and Scotland were able to operate semi-independently. The Liberal Assembly was a notoriously wayward body, combining elements both of a rally of the faithful and a policy-making body. It offered one of the more 'raw' political occasions in British politics in which giving the leadership a rough ride was almost a house sport. The Alliance with the SDP and the formation of the Liberal Democrats offered an opportunity to re-organize the Party along more modern lines. Membership was computerized and regularized so that the new Party had accurate and reliable membership figures. As important, the new Party inherited the profoundly democratic structure which had characterized the SDP, the use of ballots of members, as over the new short name of the Party and the Party leader, and a more deliberative procedure for the formulation of policy through Green and White papers. Another result was that the Liberal Assembly was replaced by a conference, now debating a fixed agenda of prepared policy documents and less subject to the one-off resolutions which had sometimes proved an embarrassment to the old Liberal leadership. But although becoming more modern and professional in its structure, the new Party retained the federal element in its constitutions which had been the hallmark of the Liberals and remained an important reflection of its commitments to federalism and regional government in Britain. Although the Party still lagged behind the two main parties in the level of resources it could command, its financial position had become more secure and predictable. From the Liberals being a party of almost legendary disorganization, the Liberal Democrats could claim to have developed an effective and modern party structure. In many respects this had been one of the most fruitful results of the merger of the SDP and the Liberal Party. The infusion of new ideas, abetted by the modernizing enthusiasm of Ashdown, had done much to create a more professional and responsible third force.

As the Liberal Democrats awaited the announcement of the calling of the next general election, they could consider themselves to have recovered from the débâcle of the post-merger period and to have re-established themselves as a third force. Poll ratings, however, still showed levels of support below those achieved by the old Alliance and the Party remained beset by calls to declare how it would behave in the event of a hung parliament, which opinion polls showed as the most likely outcome of a general election. Having recovered the position of the only effective third force in British politics, the Liberal Democrats were still seeking the chance of a decisive breakthrough which had eluded third parties since the Second World War.

The 1992 election

The Liberal Democrats entered the final six months before an election had to be called in reasonably high spirits. The sequence of by-election successes which had marked their revival after the nadir of 1988 had been confirmed by another thumping success in Scotland in Kincardine and Deeside in November 1991. Caused by the death of the popular Tory incumbent, Alick Buchanan-Smith, it was a sign of the Liberal Democrat's recovery that the seat was being written off by large sections of the press as a virtually certain Liberal Democrat gain. So it proved, with a Conservative majority of just over 2,000 turned into a Liberal Democrat majority of almost 8,000. The result was especially important for the Party in re-establishing its credentials in Scotland against the revival of the Scottish Nationalists, who came third. With the additional seat, the Liberal Democrats also overtook the Conservatives as the second-largest party in Scotland. In the two other by-elections fought on the same day, the Liberal Democrats forced the Conservatives into third place in the Labour-held Hemsworth, but were unable to make sufficient inroads into the Labour vote to do any better, nor were they able seriously to challenge a surge in Labour support which gave Labour an encouraging by-election gain at Langbaurgh.

In addition to by-election success, polling evidence showed that Paddy Ashdown entered the pre-election period with a very high level of support as leader of the Liberal Democrats. The December 1991 Gallup poll registered 58.6 per cent of the respondents as thinking he was giving the Party good leadership, a higher rating than both other party leaders. Although the Party's overall poll-ratings had slipped back from the conference-time high-points, it was still averaging 14–15 per cent at the beginning of 1992. This was less than the old Alliance, but considerably improved on the position only two years earlier. The chief obstacle to the Liberal Democrats making a greater impact lay in the revived fortunes of the Labour Party. With Labour and the Conservatives running virtually neck and neck in the polls at around 40 per cent each, the Liberal Democrats found it impossible to recapture the sort of ratings enjoyed by the Alliance in its heyday. Its relatively weaker position was shown forcefully when third-party poll ratings in the 1983–7 Parliament were compared with those achieved between 1987 and December 1991. In the former period, the Alliance had scored over 20 per cent in more than four out of five published polls taken, some 214 in all, and over 30 per cent in one in five. In the period after 1987, some 325 polls had shown the Liberal Democrats above 20 per cent in only two and at under 10 per cent in almost half. Further, if by-election evidence was taken, the Liberal Democrats were still some way off the levels of support achieved by the Alliance. In spite of the run of by-election victories since 1990, the overall picture was less convincing. In the 16 parliamentary by-elections fought between 1983 and 1987, the Alliance had averaged 39 per cent of the poll, but in the 23 between 1987 and 1992, the figure was only 20 per cent.

The inference which many commentators drew in the immediate pre-election period was that the Liberal Democrats had been steered from the brink of oblivion in 1988–9 to a position where they had become once again a force to be reckoned with, but on a more limited scale than the former Alliance. Hence the *ITN Guide* to the 1992 election, published in February 1992, opined that the Liberal Democrats were unlikely to reach the 23 per cent of the vote achieved by the Alliance in the 1987 election. The principal reason was that much of the support which the Alliance had gained in 1981–7 had come from disaffected Labour supporters, much of which had returned to Kinnock's 'new model' Labour Party and which now seemed once again a credible opposition and potential party of government. The limitations on the Liberal Democrat revival were seen in the pattern of by-election successes. In the 1987–92

Parliament the Liberal Democrat gains had been at the expense of the government in hitherto safe Conservative seats, East-bourne, Ribble Valley and Kincardine and Deeside. Although the Liberal Democrats had been able to make some inroads into a divided Labour vote at Liverpool Walton in April 1991, they had not been able to prevent Labour retaining the seat, holding Hemsworth in November or making good gains at Monmouth in June or Langbaurgh in November. Put simply, the Liberal Democrats were only doing well enough to perform the tradi-tional Liberal role of winning by-elections against an unpopular Conservative Government. What was less clear was whether when faced with a revived Labour Party at a general election they could hope to recapture the more broadly based appeal of the former Alliance and act as an effective alternative to the Labour Party for the anti-Conservative vote. On the evidence of the polls and the by-election results it appeared that Labour and the Liberal Democrats were, in effect, rival oppositions, with the added complication of the Scottish Nationalists north of the Border and Plaid Cymru in Wales also competing for the vote.

Ashdown and the Liberal Democrats could, however, stress more positive aspects. Past experience had shown that pre-election polls tended to underestimate the Liberal Democrat vote. Time and time again, expert predictions had been con-founded by much heavier support than anticipated for the third force. While some commentators felt that breaking the 20 per cent barrier was unlikely, it was recognized that the Liberal Democrats could well increase the number of their seats by concentrating on specific targets. A 5 per cent decline in share of the vote in the 1991 council elections had still brought the Liberal Democrats over 500 gains through effective targetting. The Liberal Democrat's position as the main challenger in a swathe of some 20 seats where a swing of only 4 per cent would net them the victory, offered the alluring prospect of an increase in the number of seats even if the share of the vote was less than that achieved by the Alliance in 1983 and 1987. If, as many Liberal Democrats hoped, they could capitalize on Conservative disaffection and raise their share of the vote back to former

Alliance levels or even better, the prospect of a genuine breakthrough was not impossible.

Ashdown, himself, in private briefings as late as January 1992 was ready to play down expectations for the forthcoming election. His message was that the real prospects for his Party lay in the election after next, either as a result of a hung Parliament or as a result of a further Labour defeat which would see Labour either torn apart in internecine strife or, at the very least, ready to accept electoral reform. With all the opinion polls making a hung Parliament or a very small Conservative majority the most likely outcome of the election, these were not unrealistic projections. Publicly, however, the pre-election calculations were disrupted in early February by the revelation of Ashdown's past affair with a former secretary, prior to his election as leader of the Party. For a moment it appeared that the Liberal Democrats were faced with a nightmare replay of the Thorpe affair of the early 1970s in which a personal scandal would destroy a promising leader. However, Ashdown moved swiftly and decisively both the limit the damage and to turn the tables on the press for attempting a 'dirty tricks' campaign. He was able to relegate the issue to a phase of his past, stress its entirely personal character and as having nothing to do with current politics. Widely perceived as having come out of a difficult situation well, Ashdown and the Liberal Democrats saw a surge in their support in the polls just as the long 'phoney election' campaign was drawing to a close.

Thus, when John Major called an election for 9 April, the Liberal Democrats already felt themselves on an upward tide of support. Moreover, the objective position of the Government had worsened. The recovery still seemed a distant prospect, unemployment and bankruptcies were still rising and the expected increase in Conservative support from Chancellor Lamont's budget had not materialized. The odds appeared to be moving increasingly from a reduced Conservative majority to one in which a hung Parliament was becoming increasingly likely. The Liberal Democrats' manifesto showed few surprises, but it became clear that the main emphasis of the campaign was to be the dramatic pledge of the Party to place 1p on the standard rate of income tax to fund an increase in spending on education and training. In what was largely perceived as a negative campaign, Ashdown was also able to make considerable capital out of 'a plague on both their houses' approach, emphasized by the almost farcical disputes between the two main parties over Labour's attempt to present a real case of health-service failure in one of its party political broadcasts. A carefully-planned strategy of not committing the party to support either side but to await the outcome of the election allowed Ashdown to deflect the questions which had affected the 1987 Alliance campaign. Repeated almost *ad nauseam*, Ashdown's stock formulation was that it was up to other Party leaders to recognize the wishes of the people if they voted for a 'balanced Parliament' and to seek co-operation with the Liberal Democrats to produce a period of stable government. He left it in little doubt, however, that the price for Liberal Democrat support would be a commitment to proportional representation.

On the face of it, the Liberal Democrat campaign was a success. Ashdown's energetic criss-crossing of the country, firm spending commitments on education and offer to participate in any coalition which would produce a stable platform for recovery and electoral reform seemed to present a coherent message. The electorate appeared to be responding, the polls showing an increase in Liberal Democrat support during the campaign. Three out of the four polls taken in the final week of the campaign showed Liberal Democrat support at 20 per cent. Most remarkable of all, the last weekend of the campaign was dominated by the constitutional issue in an atmosphere in which every poll pointed to an indecisive outcome. Kinnock was forced to edge nearer the Liberal Democrats, offering them a place on the Labour Party's Plant Commission on electoral reform in what were widely regarded as the first moves in post-election manoeuvring between Labour and the Liberal Democrats. For their part, the Conservatives were forced into ever more vehement defence of the constitutional status quo, launching an attack on proportional representation as likely to produce unstable governments. For the first time ever electoral reform was actually an issue in a general election.

As the ballot boxes were being sealed and despatched for the counts, the Liberal Democrats had much to be satisfied with. The long pre-election period since Major's assumption of the premiership had given the Liberal Democrats the opportunity to activate a twenty-member election planning group set up as early as June 1990 under the experienced Des Wilson as Campaign Co-ordinator. The plan for the campaign had been followed fairly closely: the utilization of Ashdown's fitness and energy for a barnstorming progress through the country; the attempt to stand above the political slanging of the other two parties; the concentration on a set of high-profile issues, such as education and economic recovery; emphasis on the potential of a Liberal Democrat vote to anticipate charges of a 'wasted' vote from the other parties; and the establishment of proportional representation as a major issue in the public mind. Apart from one or two minor 'wobbles' when individuals had departed from the carefully-formulated responses on major issues during the campaign, the plan had been fulfilled far beyond expectations. There was little more the Party could have done by way of preparation and while elements of the campaign could be questioned, few objective commentators felt at the time that it had been anything other than a success. It was undoubtedly the case that early planning had allowed a slicker, more professional campaign, moreover one produced on a fraction of the budget of the larger parties. Above all, the Party had been able to reap the benefit of the painful merger process and speak with one voice to the electorate. Even at the price of a somewhat monotonous repetition by Ashdown of the stock formulae about what the Liberal Democrats would do following an indecisive result, the Party was able to avoid the worst features of the 'two-headed' campaign in 1987.

Moreover, the Liberal Democrats in England had a clear run as *the* third party with an allocation of air-time in ratio to the other two parties which, as ever, raised their profile with the electorate. While as late as January 1992 there were many who were still confused about the identity of the merged Party, media attention on Ashdown's personal affairs, followed by the election campaign, greatly enhanced the Party's visibility. As striking was the failure of any other minor party to make an impact.

Although the Greens put up over 200 candidates, their campaign was undermined from the outset by a decline in support since the Euro-elections of 1989, internal divisions and lack of funds. However important as an issue, the Green challenge barely surfaced in the campaign. Nor did that of the band of 'old Liberals' opposed to the merger and inspired by Michael Meadowcroft who fought in over 70 seats. The former SDP was now represented by only two sitting MPs, Rosie Barnes and John Cartwright, the latter even being endorsed by the Liberal Democrats. Having decided not to contest his Plymouth seat, David Owen remained alienated from the main campaign, though making a late intervention on behalf of John Major. Only in Scotland, where the Scottish Nationalist Party had generated considerable support during the campaign, did the intervention of another force seriously threaten the Liberal Democrats, squeezing their support in the polls carried out prior to election day.

The results, when announced, proved a disappointment. Behind the headline of a Conservative overall majority of 21 seats, the Liberal Democrats had secured just 20 seats on the basis of 18.3 per cent of the vote. Overall, the total vote was more than a million down on what the Alliance had achieved in 1987. The by-election gains of 1990–1 at Eastbourne, Ribble Valley and Kincardine and Deeside were lost as well as three gains in 1987. While the Party did well in the South-West winning back Devon North and Cornwall North, they lost Southport and two seats in Wales. The Party had been able to take only two of its target seats, Cheltenham and Bath, but missed four others by less than a thousand votes, two of which, Portsmouth South and Stockton South, required swings of less than 1 per cent. Instead, in the latter, the Party came in third. Other three-way marginals proved equally unhappy, the Party finishing in third place in Edinburgh West, Colne Valley and two of the Plymouth divisions. If the overall tally of seats and missed opportunities was discouraging, the Labour Party's advance, although inadequate to secure victory, had been sufficient to push them into second place in another 75 seats, putting them second in 186 compared to 145 for the Liberal

Democrats. Even in the midst of Labour's dismay at a fourth election defeat in a row, the reality was that Labour had made significant gains overall and pushed themselves into a more challenging position than previously in much of Southern England. Most disheartening of all, the prospect of a hung Parliament, viewed almost as a certainty right up to polling day and predicted in the exit polls announced on election night, vanished like a mirage once the real results began to come in. As election night wore on the Conservative's unexpected triumph deprived the Liberal Democrats of any role to play in the formation of the next government.

In fact, the gains and losses for the Liberal Democrats in the 1992 election were nicely balanced. Ashdown struck a bullish note in his immediate post-election pronouncement. The result, he argued, confirmed that Labour could not win power on its own. Even with a recession and the legacy of the Poll Tax, Labour had only been able to obtain 35 per cent of all votes cast. Labour's attempt to prove itself a viable alternative government in its own right looked shattered. Second, Ashdown was able to reinforce the traditional message about the unfairness of the electoral system. The Liberal Democrats had been 'cheated' by the result which under a PR system with their share of the vote, would have earned them over a hundred seats. As ever, millions of votes had brought them only a fraction of the seats of the other two parties. It had taken almost 300,000 votes to elect each Liberal Democrat MP, compared with just over 40,000 for each Labour and Conservative member. These arguments had great relevance in a context where prominent Labour spokesmen, such as Robin Cook, were quick to point out that the Conservatives had once again taken power on a minority of the popular vote. Under PR, the Conservatives would only have been the largest party, more than 80 seats short of an overall majority. Instead, with just 11 seats won on majorities ranging from 19 to 585 votes, a total of under 3,000 votes, making all the difference, the first-past-the-post system had given the Conservatives up to five years more of undisputed power.

It was this indirect effect upon the Labour Party, pushing them further down the road towards proportional representation which looked the most promising outcome for the Liberal Democrats. Some Labour supporters were even prepared to talk about the possibility of pacts, although significant doubts remained as to whether such deals were actually feasible. Less likely was the major realignment of the left which Ashdown and earlier Liberal and Alliance supporters have looked for. Even in its evident dismay at failing for a fourth time, Labour could seek comfort in the large gains it had made. The 'one last heave' argument, combined with criticism of aspects of the Labour Party's tactics in the campaign which might be avoided next time, suggested that Labour was unlikely to abandon its role as the major party of opposition. What seemed most likely was that a Labour Party pledged to electoral reform would at least be able to make common cause with the Liberal Democrats on constitutional issues, offering the prospect in the medium term of the changed electoral system for which the Party had campaigned for so long.

What was also clear was that the next election was almost bound to be fought on the first-past-the-post system. In the immediate term, the prospects were mixed. The Party had gained members during the campaign, was in a reasonably good financial position and was unified behind its leader. The Greens and 'old Liberal' rivals had performed badly, while the election had also seen the removal of the last two SDP MPs. On the other hand, the electoral geography looked distinctly less promising for the Liberal Democrats on at least two counts. First, they were in second place in only 11 seats where the Conservative majority was under 4,000, compared with Labour's 42, making prospects for a rapid increase in seats unlikely. Second, the 1992 election result seemed to stem from a last-minute flight of support from the Liberal Democrats to the Conservatives as prospects of a Labour victory or of a hung Parliament became more likely. There was an evident danger that pro-Conservative voters who were prepared to flirt with the Liberal Democrats might be alienated by too close a relationship with Labour.

For the Liberal Democrats, the 1992 election seemed to offer a range of possibilities. In hindsight, its most important feature was the re-establishment of the Party as a viable third force after the traumas of merger. Compared with the low point of its fortunes in 1988, 20 MPs, over 100,000 members and the almost certain conversion of one of the other large parties to proportional representation seemed a pretty good outcome. The larger hopes of the third force, however, those of Grimond, the early Alliance leaders and of Ashdown himself, for a major realignment of the left in which Labour would be replaced by the Liberal Democrats as the main opposition, still looked a long way off.

7 Conclusion

In the considerable political turmoil after the 1987 election, the prospect for a third force in British politics had been dramatically reshaped. The old Liberal Party had, in fact, ceased to exist, ending its long independent history and merging its identity along with the majority of the activists, councillors and MPs, of the seven-year-old SDP in the Social and Liberal Democrats. What the future holds is difficult to predict, but a review of the strengths and weaknesses of the Liberal Party revealed by its history since 1945 suggests some pointers for third-party politics in general.

First, the survival of the Liberal Party to become a major component of a new political party was not a foregone conclusion. Its revival from near-extinction in the immediate post-war years represents one of the most remarkable political comebacks of the century. In a reversal of the process of apparently ineluctable decline witnessed for much of the first half of the century, the record since 1955 has been of revival, if not to its pre-1914 strength, then well beyond that prior to 1945. Second, the history of the Liberal Party, the Alliance and the Liberal Democrats demonstrates the disadvantage of any third party in Britain under the present electoral system. Although the Alliance obtained approximately a quarter of all votes cast in 1983 and 1987, it obtained only a score or more Members of Parliament. The problem of a first-past-the-post system for any minority party was compounded by the even spread and volatility of its support, so that it was unable to count upon a bloc of 'safe' seats in the way Labour did in its industrial heartlands or the

Conservatives did in the South of England. Even if the Labour party's support fell dramatically at some future general election it would still have scores of MPs because of the concentration of its electoral support. In so far as the Liberal Party and its successors have had any bastions they have tended to remain the traditional Liberal areas of the Celtic fringe and the more rural parts of Britain. In spite of a broadening of their electoral base after the 1960s, the Liberal Democrats still, as late as the 1992 election, drew a disproportionate number of its MPs from South-West England, Wales and Scotland. Even so, there was no seat which the Liberals and their successors could claim to have held permanently this century.

Third, any minority party working within the adversarial tradition of British politics, where the role of government and opposition is enshrined in the procedures of Parliament, now emphasized by television, and reinforced in the attitudes of the media, operates at a disadvantage. The Liberal party and then the Alliance were dependent upon by-election successes to raise its public visibility and earn it the media attention it otherwise lacks. As a third party operating in a two-party situation, the Liberals and their successors have frequently found themselves denied the 'oxygen of publicity' which any modern party requires and gasping for air in the lulls between by-elections. This has led many to the conclusion that it is only by replacing one of the other major parties that any third force can achieve a breakthrough.

Certainly at parliamentary level, the fortunes of the Liberal Party can be shown to have been dependent in large part upon the state of the other parties. The Liberal revival took off in the late fifties amidst the disillusion with the Conservative Government of Macmillan; its point of greatest, if illusory, success came when both major parties were in the doldrums in the early eighties. At one level, third-party fortunes have oscillated most directly in relationship to the position of the governing party of the day. The Liberals, the Alliance and then the Liberal Democrats have frequently seen a revival begin two or three years into a government. The latest Liberal Democrat revival in the polls and at by-elections in the autumn and winter of

1990–1 drew heavily upon the severe unpopularity of the Conservatives over the economy, Europe and the Poll Tax. No third party, however, competing against two larger parliamentary parties in the first-past-the-post system was invulnerable to a squeeze operated against them. Even as the Liberal Democrats attempted to re-establish the credibility of a third force, there was always the threat that a revival of more centrist policies in both major parties might still operate to depress their share of the vote and deny them a significant body of votes and seats.

But, fourth, it was easy to forget that the first-past-the-post system also operated in favour of the Liberals and, later, the Alliance in allowing it to remain the most significant third party. The political system which imposed minority status on the Liberal Party, also imposed a difficult threshold for other parties to cross in obtaining MPs and significant local representation. Apart from the regionally-based Nationalist parties, other potential third and fourth parties, such as the National Front, the various left-wing groups, the Greens and the continuing SDP were unable to mount an effective challenge for third-party status. The Liberals and the Alliance started with a major advantage over the others, they inherited the tradition of an established party, had a national organization and a recognized place in the political firmament. The Liberals might complain of being disadvantaged in terms of media coverage and the procedures of Parliament, but while they retained even a handful of seats in Parliament they were accorded at least some of the attention and privileges denied to those still trying to break into the system. The threshold of support and credibility which was required to elect even one MP in an English constituency was one which most minor parties found too high to cross. The Liberals remained over that threshold, perilously in the 1950s, more securely thereafter. What the Nationalists proved able to achieve in Scotland and Wales from the 1970s, proved virtually impossible for any of the other forces competing for attention in England. Neither the extreme left nor the extreme right, numerically the largest challengers in the 1970s, were able to break into Parliament. Nor was the Ecology Party and its successor, the Green Party, able to achieve parliamentary success. Whether the SDP after 1981 would have been able to achieve such a breakthrough on its own is difficult to determine because it almost immediately became part of the Alliance with the Liberals. The high public profile of its leadership and the febrile political climate of the early 1980s might suggest that if the Alliance had not been formed, the Liberals would have had a serious contender for third-party status. Things might have been different. If the MPs who joined the SDP as sitting Labour and Conservative MPs had resigned *en masse* and sought re-election in the propitious circumstances of 1981, it is possible that the SDP's strength within the Alliance might have remained higher in 1983 and 1987 than it in fact did. By 1987 the SDP had been whittled down to five seats in its own right and was outnumbered by the Liberals. Whatever the intentions of the Alliance partners, the effect was that the Liberals allied with and then ultimately merged with the only force that might have been an effective contender for third-party status.

Fifth, an encouraging feature of the political situation for the Liberal Democrats as they emerged from the merger process was that party dealignment was providing a 'space' in which a third party could reach and sustain a respectable proportion of the popular vote. The crushing duopoly of the decade immediately after the Second World War did not look like returning. The high Liberal share of the vote in February 1974, a fifth, and the two Alliance elections of 1983 and 1987, seemed to confirm that levels of third-party and other support were generally higher. Although the Liberals and later the SLD were to see their opinion poll ratings plummet to low single figures, no election since 1959 had seen the total share of the vote for third and other parties combined fall below 10 per cent and since 1974 below 18 per cent. Within that period the Liberals had fallen as low as 7.5 per cent of the vote as late as 1970, but this still compared favourably with the situation in the decade after the Second World War. Moreover, although the number of seats won was much smaller than the proportion of the popular vote, the Alliance in particular had built up its position as the second party to the Conservatives in a large number of seats in

Southern England. After 1987 the Liberal Democrats were the main challengers in approximately a third of the Conservative marginals. Even with Labour's advance in 1992, there were a large number of seats, 145 in all, where the Liberal Democrats were in second place. In effect, in a large number of seats the third force was the major opposition party. This shift in the electoral geography remained somewhat in the balance while the merged Party found its feet after the wreck of the Alliance. But, as the Liberal Democrats established themselves and saw off the challenge of the continuing SDP and the Greens, it looked as though the Party's position in Southern England had taken on a more permanent character. This was confirmed in 1992 when at the general election the Liberal Democrats took a higher share of the vote than Labour in the South-West and in the South-East, excluding Greater London. This apparently expanded base in the electoral and political spectrum had probably antedated the 1979 election. According to one influential analysis, there was evidence the Liberal Party was gradually acquiring a more visible identity in the 1970s and had thus been exerting a greater 'pull' on the electorate.[1] The increased pull was assisted further by the formation of the Alliance. Although it is impossible to determine whether further defection to the Liberals would have occurred in any case even if the Social Democratic party had not broken from Labour, there was little doubt that the Liberal Democrats were, after the hiatus of the merger talks and their immediate aftermath, able to pick up where the Alliance had left off.

Sixth, the achievement of a degree of credibility by the successors to the Alliance was crucial for them to capitalize on the other features of the electoral sociology of Britain from the late 1960s, which was a degree of electoral volatility. 'Volatility' is a term which needs handling with care; some aspects of electoral behaviour were less volatile than they had been in the past. There were fewer marginal seats, for example, perhaps half as many as in the 1950s, and recent research has suggested that structural dealignment of Labour and Conservative has had a less important part to play than short-term fluctuations in the popularity and performance of governments. But elements of volatility have entered into the political scene in other ways. Even those who have qualified the theory of greater volatility on the part of the electorate most heavily, have accepted that one of the features of electoral change since the 1970s has been a small, but expanding base for the Liberals, and, later, the Alliance.[2] Also, as David Butler has pointed out, the record of by-elections has shown greater volatility: between 1945 and 1965 only 8 per cent of by-elections led to a change in party control, but between 1966 and 1987 the figure was 30 per cent.[3] Huge switches of support against incumbent governments became a more common feature of British politics, from Orpington down to Ribble Valley, with the third party often the principal beneficiary. Support for major parties in the polls also showed a greater degree of fluctuation over the course of the post-war period and with it the capacity for the third party to make sudden surges in popularity. The 40–50 per cent support being shown for the Alliance at its formation was a symptom of this, but so was the sudden rise in the popularity of the Greens from almost nowhere to poll ratings ahead of the Liberal Democrats and an unprecedented surge to 15 per cent of the vote in the Euro-elections. The loss of mid-term by-election gains in subsequent general elections and the often sudden reduction in poll ratings witnessed by the Alliance and the Greens, as well as by Nationalist parties, have reinforced the dimensions of considerable and growing volatility.

The survival of a viable third party and electoral volatility were mutually reinforcing. From an early stage the Liberals provided a home for protest votes, amounting to up to half their vote in the general election of the late 1950s, giving their electoral support a transient quality. Relatively few Liberal voters were loyal to the Liberals from one election to another and compared with the Conservatives and Labour Party the Liberals had more temporary adherents. Studies of Alliance support in the 1980s also suggest that there was less close identification of Alliance voters with their party than existed for the main parties. The Alliance vote was notoriously 'soft'. It put on and lost support in short order with a high turnover from one election to another. Two factors which had begun to operate by the mid-1980s, however, were the beginning of an expansion of a 'harder' Alliance vote, especially among middle-class salaried and professional groups, as well as the increasing number of electors prepared to cast their vote for a third party. Greater education, social change, political failures by both major parties and the growing influence of the media seemed to be creating an ever larger potential catchment area for a third force. Whether more than a decade of Conservative rule after 1979 and a refurbishment of Labour's policies and image from 1983 would reduce this catchment area remained to be tested in a subsequent general election. There was evidence, however, from the Ribble Valley by-election of March 1991 that the Liberal Democrats had retained the ability to act as the focus for massive disapproval with a sitting government's performance. As significant was an exit poll which showed that had it been a general election the seat would have been held by the Conservatives. None the less, the ability of a third party like the Liberal Democrats to win in such circumstances continued to have the effect of reinforcing their standing in the polls and their wider credibility.

Seventh, it was becoming apparent by the 1980s that routine polling often proved a poor guide to election performance for third parties. At the end of May 1983, the Alliance stood at 17 per cent in Gallup, but polled a full eight points more in the general election on 9 June. The 1979 election had also seen a late swing to the Liberals which took their position from a polling position of 9 per cent at the calling of the election to nearly 14 per cent of the actual poll. Both at by-elections and at the annual May council elections, there was evidence of the third party consistently outmatching the expectations of pollsters. It became almost a cliché of Alliance spokespersons in the 1980s that 'real' votes tended to be far more favourable to the third party than routine statements of voting intention. The bandwagon effects of third-party campaigning, especially in by-elections at which the Liberals and the Alliance became expert practitioners, as well as in some general election campaigns, always seemed to offer the prospect of a larger breakthrough than experts anticipated and generated its own momentum and excitement. Thus, even while relegated to minority status by all the usual indices, the third party always had the self-fulfilling potential for a major upset.

Eighth, the growing volatility of the electorate has been compounded by the issue of tactical voting. Increasing evidence that better-informed voters were beginning to place their vote where it had the best chance of being effective rather than voting automatically for their candidate of first preference, offered alluring prospects for a third party which held second place in a large number of seats. This was exactly the position in which the Alliance found itself in 1987 and which the Liberal Democrats inherited thereafter. During the 1987 election it was shown by John Curtice and Michael Steed that many Labour voters switched their votes to the Alliance where they could see their own preferred candidate having no chance of winning. The effect varied across Britain, but in the North and West it was big enough to add an extra 5 per cent to the Alliance vote where the Alliance was well ahead of Labour. There was less evidence of it where the Alliance and Labour were more closely matched and in the South and East of Britain the additional Alliance vote was much less.[4] There was speculation that if 1987 proved a paradigm and the electorate had become more acclimatized to the idea of using their vote with discretion, to which the by-elections at Eastbourne, Ribble Valey and Kincardine and Deeside could be seen as confirmation, then the Liberal Democrats had the opportunity to increase their number of seats. Calculations suggested that if the degree of tactical voting seen in the North and West in 1987 was to occur in the South and East, it would lead to Liberal Democrat gains. A study of the marginal constituencies after the 1987 election suggested that a greater concentration of the tactical vote behind the Liberal Democrats could mean them gaining proportionately more seats on a lower share of the poll.[5] This outcome was confirmed in the 1992 election, where on a reduced poll compared with 1987, the Liberal Democrats were only two seats down. There was considerable evidence that Labour voters had been prepared to back Liberal Democrat candidates to unseat the Conservatives. While frequently unsuccessful, it suggested the potential for the third party to benefit from its possible attraction to voters whose own candidates were in a hopeless position. There was also the danger that Liberal Democrat supporters might 'peel off' to support other parties, a particular threat to a party with attractions to both potential Labour and Conservative voters. According to one exit poll in 1992, about a third of Liberal Democrat supporters had voted tactically for other parties, a factor which allowed Labour some higher than average swings in marginals, but also saw some rallying of support behind the Conservatives. As a result, the Liberal Democrats are not the unmitigated beneficiaries of tactical voting. What it offers is the potential for third-party support where the electorate can identify with it as the principal means of unseating an incumbent. In effect, it operates under the present electoral system as a crude form of proportional representation, often, but by no means always, to the benefit of the Liberal Democrats.

A further factor which has helped to alter the political situation since 1945 is the establishment of the third-party presence in local government. With over 3,000 local councillors, the Liberal Democrats and former Alliance have been successful in establishing an apparently permanent power base in local government in both rural and urban areas. SLD councillors have controlled areas as diverse as Tower Hamlets in London, Stockport, Hereford, Plymouth and Blyth Valley in the Northeast. In an even larger number of counties they have held the balance of power. Moreover, there is a clear discrepancy between local election results and national opinion polls; they tend to be more favourable to a third force than answers to pollsters would indicate. This was critical in allowing the SLD to survive the trauma of merger. By May 1991 good local election results allowed the heirs of the Alliance to improve their position still further. Here again, credibility was at stake. Unlike the position in the 1950s, the Alliance and the SLD were able increasingly to become a winning force in local government. Though still patchy in representation and in a minority overall, the ability of the third party to build on local successes and to translate them into winning positions in by-elections and general elections was another factor in the weakening of two-party control.

Finally, what of policy? Since 1945 the Liberal Party has always found it difficult to establish an identity sufficiently distinctive from that of the two major parties. Even when its revival began in the late fifties it was easy to argue that it was no more than a 'protest' party and as recently as the 1987 election one of the commonest complaints of electors was that they did not know what the Alliance stood for. In many ways, however, the Party has been more important as a source of ideas which have entered the mainstream of political debate than as a vehicle for carrying them out. Liberals have variously championed devolution and regional government, industrial partnership, a Bill of Rights, equal pay for women, freedom of information, reform of the House of Lords, entry to the Common Market, environmental protection, reform of the domestic rating system and proportional representation. A glance at this list illustrates a common problem, that other parties could easily adopt third-party policies and adapt them to their own purposes. Of the few distinct ideas that had *not* been taken-up by another party, the principal one remained proportional representation with which even the Labour Party was beginning to flirt as another general election approached in 1992. With no copyright on ideas, however, any third party always remained exposed to the danger of having its clothes stolen by other parties. These threats became acute in the run-up to the 1992 election as both other parties converged upon the centre ground. Labour was now multilateralist, pro-European, in favour of a Freedom of Information Act, had coherent proposals for regional government, including a Scottish Assembly, and had abandoned old-style nationalization. Under their new leader, John Major, the Conservatives had, after some delay, ditched the Poll Tax, softened their position on Europe and issued a 'Citizen's Charter'. It was difficult in these circumstances for the new Liberal Democrats to create a distinctive identity. Ashdown attempted to do so by once again asserting the radical position previously claimed by earlier Liberal leaders.

In practice, the old Liberal Party and then the Alliance had been more important as a vehicle for putting ideas on the political agenda than their direct influence on government would suggest. In part this derived from what hostile commentators saw as a position of irresponsibility. The Liberal Party could afford the luxury of adopting any number of policy proposals which it would never have to implement in practice. Such charges were not entirely fair as all parties have saddled themselves with policies either in government or in opposition which have caused or would have caused very serious practical difficulties. The Labour manifesto of 1983 and the Conservative Poll Tax legislation were but two examples of major parties adopting policies at the margins of credibility and public acceptance. What is striking is how many are what would later become mainstream concerns: the environment, individual liberties and citizen's rights, the Common Market, the reduction of the role of central government and devolution and the adoption of more democratic political structures were first taken up by the third party. Undoubtedly, for a time, the Liberal Party operated as a kind of informal 'think-tank' where ideas currently on the horizon of public consciousness often got their first airing. The formation of the SDP and the Alliance also gave opportunities for a fresh input of ideas. One at least was to create a model of party structure which was more democratic in procedures and policy formulation than either of the other two major parties. Moreover, where the Liberal Party had been able to assert influence in the past it had supported issues of a traditional Liberal nature, such as David Steel's sponsoring of the Abortion Act in 1967 and the promotion of a housing Bill for the homeless and employee share ownership under the Lib-Lab pact. In general terms the pressing need to define a distinct identity has forced the third party to explore more actively issues and policies which were novel and distinctive.

The question of policy goes to the heart of a major dilemma facing the Liberal Democrats as a third force; the question of their identity and whether they are a radical or a centre party. Ever since Jo Grimond set out to give the Party a distinctive place in the political spectrum as a non-socialist radical party, it has remained the preferred position to which successive third-party leaders have returned. Although 'radical' was a term guaranteed to raise applause at a Liberal Assembly where it conjured up the Party's nineteenth-century inheritance of the attack on entrenched privilege and power, it was one subject to a variety of meanings by the latter part of the twentieth century. Indeed, it was one which by the 1960s might as easily be understood as meaning simply left wing, identified with the extreme left and a revolutionary re-distribution of wealth and power. Yet again, in Thatcherite hands, it came to be identified with the tough-minded, free-market, non-interventionist ethos of the 'new right'. If Tony Benn was a radical and Keith Joseph was a radical, where exactly did the Liberal Party stand when it used the term to describe itself?

This confusion is largely explained by the inadequacy of political vocabulary to account for complex and multi-variate ideological and policy positions. A favoured resolution for it in recent years has come through the use of the term 'progressive' rather than 'radical'. The idea of progressivism harks back to the period before the Great War when the Liberal Party began to amend the ideological consistency of pure laissez-faire Liberalism to allow a greater degree of state intervention over social welfare and embarked on major constitutional reform, notably reform of the House of Lords and Irish Home Rule. What it offered was a reconcilation of major reform, even that requiring state intervention and permanently enhanced responsibilities for government, with the preservation of a libertarian ethos and free-market economics. It thus took up a reforming stance which was distinct from that of the traditional socialist left with their commitments to a socialized economy and central planning. Equally, it was distinct from the party of the right, the Conservatives, and their support for the status quo and the preservation of the existing distribution of power. It was this which allowed Liberal leaders such as Grimond, then the founders of the SDP, and latterly Ashdown to use the language of radicalism while distancing themselves from the traditional socialist agenda. In its most sophisticated formulations, it has been seen as a reclaiming of a radical progressivism of the early twentieth century, a progressive spirit which Labour had initially shared but which had increasingly been stifled by labourism and centralizing socialism. For the electorate, however, such a rationale was not an easy one to explain in terms of conventional views of a simple left-right polarization.

This potential confusion was compounded by the paradoxical position the third force often found itsself in of seeking to replace the Labour Party as the principal party of opposition and the kind of voters the party has attracted. The Liberal Party found it much easier to achieve by-election successes by winning over disaffected Conservatives than traditional Labour voters. Similarly, when the Alliance aimed to capitalize on an exceptional period of Labour disarray and to replace it, the results were disappointing. By 1987, of the 22 seats held by the Liberal/SDP Alliance, 16 had the Conservatives in second place – if they could be construed as 'natural' territory for any other party it would have been the Conservatives. Strikingly, 13 of the seats lay in rural Wales and Scotland, and three more in the West Country. Similarly, the list of the 22 most marginal seats in which the Liberal Democrats were in contention after 1987 contained 14 Conservative seats. The dilemma has been expressed simply in the terms that there is a clear conflict between securing the maximum number of Liberal Democrat MPs and the longer-term aim of trying to replace Labour as the Conservatives' principal opponents.[6] Short-term aims of having sufficient MPs to wield influence and improve credibility are at cross-purposes with the professed long-term aim of becoming the major opposition party. But there was no doubting that this would remain the position for the foreseeable future. It has been notable that at no time have Liberal, Alliance or Liberal Democrat leaders ever espoused publicly the aim, not of replacing Labour, but of replacing the Conservatives. The commitment to being a party of reform, even radical reform, is so ingrained that the Party has had no choice but to live with this problem.

If electoral considerations complicated the third party's search for a place for itself in the political spectrum, so, too, did speculations about the prospects for a hung Parliament and how the party would deal with the outcome. As Grimond and

Thorpe had found as Liberal leaders, and Steel and Owen as Alliance leaders, the question of which party they would support and the conditions they would exact for it were potentially divisive. Indeed, the very concentration of the media on the question of how the party stood in such circumstances tended to emphasize a lack of clear identity. It was not an easy dilemma to escape from: a stated preference for either main party threatened to alienate existing activists and supporters and, even more seriously, discourage potential voters from the other parties. Attempts to keep options open always carried the danger of charges of lack of principle, incoherence and inconsistency. When the Party prepared for the 1992 election, these questions wre met by an attempt to mark out a distinctive agenda which was more radical than Labour on constitutional and environmental matters and more free-market orientated on aspects of the economy than the Conservatives. This was combined with commitments to further spending on education and raising taxes if necessary to fund it. With pro-federal Europeanism balanced by support for regional devolution and support for multilateralism, the Liberal Democrats could fairly claim not to fit neatly into any simple ideological category. On the whole, however, it looked like the Party was positioning itself more on the reforming and progressive wing of policies, a stance that included a strong dose of laissez-faire in such matters as monopolies and wage-bargaining. The issue of what the Party would do in a hung or as the Liberal Democrats preferred to call it, a 'balanced' Parliament, was answered by emphasis on a commitment to proportional representation, even if this meant a second election. Talk of any pre-election deals with either party was discounted. Ashdown's attempts to steer clear of the minefield of confusion which had affected the 1987 campaign met with reasonable success during the campaign. There was a strong suggestion, however, that in the final days the electrorate's perception of a hung Parliament as unstable and unwelcome, particularly in the midst of a recession, undermined Liberal Democrat support.

Looking to the longer term, the Party could hope that the further Labour defeat inflicted in 1992 would lead ultimately to electoral reform. What remained less clear and less considered, was how Liberal Democrats would fare once proportional representation was achieved. What direction would they take on policy matters, particularly on the economy and the role of government, in the major welfare debates, on defence and on the environment? In particular, the ability of the Party to act as the focus for a range of groups opposed to the other two parties might be compromised by the freedom for further party formation which proportional representation might bring. Where earlier elections on first-past-the-post had severely limited the potential for rival parties to steal the Liberal's status as the only effective third party and where, as recently as 1992, the Greens, old Liberals and others had been unable to elect members, electoral reform might allow a greater plurality of parties to gain seats. Would Britain follow the model of PR systems such as those of Ireland or Germany with fairly stable third parties or would the glue which had held the third force together unstick in a welter of minor parties?

The outright Conservative victory in 1992 has undoubtedly postponed electoral reform for the immediate future. A divided opposition to the Tories as in 1983 and 1987 leaves them as a clear majority party. It has been argued that their position is becoming analagous to that of 'dominant party' systems such as are found in Japan or, until recently, in Sweden. The Liberal Democrat role in such a position is almost bound to be one of seeking some common cause with the other opposition party, though full-scale realignment of the opposition looks unlikely. Labour would certainly prefer the development and continuation of a 'two-and-a-half-party' system in which Consrvatives and Labour continue to function as the only potential parties of government. This looks increasingly less likely in view of Labour's fourth defeat and its overall electoral postiion. Boundary Commission changes threaten to make a Labour victory at the next election much harder to achieve. With only 35 per cent of the vote in 1992, a further loss of seats looming through boundary changes and a favourable electoral opportunity lost, Labour has come close to losing its status as an alternative governing party. The widespread question, heard on previous occasions, of 'Can Labour ever win again?' now has an increasing ring of conviction.

In general terms, this puts the future of a classic 'two-party' system very much in the balance. But it is worth reflecting that the British political system has always contained the potential for third-party complication. Indeed, it has been argued that a two-party Conservative–Labour system has never really existed in Britain. At no point since 1918 has Labour, as main opposition party, succeeded in displacing the Liberals from potential command of a basic 15 per cent of the national vote. The Liberals themselves artificially depressed their vote, by entering basically Conservative Governments, through their own divisions and splits, and by not putting up candidates in many seats. In the 1930s, for example, they had joined the Conservative-dominated National Government and campaigned in only a fifth of seats. After 1945 the number of candidates was frequently so low as to depress their position artificially. In support of this Patrick Dunleavy has shown that in the 20 general elections since 1918, when the three main parties first competed against each other, the average Liberal or Alliance vote has been 13 per cent, ranging between a high point of 30 per cent in 1923 and a low point of 2.5 per cent in 1951. Six of these election scores are in the 5–10 per cent range and four in the 20–30 per cent range. But these figures understated underlying levels of Libral support because of the failure to put forward candidates in elections in the 1930s and the 1950s. A more accurate measure of third-party support lies in the *votes per candidate* since 1922, when a more stable level of third-party support emerges. In seats where they fielded candidates, the average Liberal/Alliance vote was 19 per cent, the highest 38 per cent and the lowest 12 per cent. Eight of the election scores have been in the range of 15–20 per cent.[7] Providing the Liberal Democrats can field a full slate of candidates, as they were able to do in 1992, it is more likely that they will poll at least 15 per cent of the vote. The Liberal Democrats, in other words, have proved able to capture the 'normal' potential level of third-party support. The implications of this for the other parties are substantial, particularly in closely fought elections. The Liberal Democrats might assist the Conservatives by dividing the opposition vote in crucial marginals that Labour has to win, but fail to take their own targets and thus enhance prospects for a

Conservative majority. On the other hand, a good Liberal Democrat performance taking seats from the Conservatives in areas where Labour has no chance of doing so might contribute substantially to a Conservative defeat. The role of the third party will remain, it appears, a major factor in the political future of Britain.

Notes

1 A. Heath, R. Jowell and J. Curtice, *How Britain Votes* (Pergamon, Oxford, 1985), pp. 150–2.
2 *Ibid.*, pp. 142–6, 171, 175.
3 D. Butler, *British General Elections since 1945*, (Basil Blackwell, Oxford, 1989), pp. 63–7.
4 G. Smyth (ed.), *Can the Tories Lose? The Battle for the Marginals*, (Lawrence and Wishart, London, 1991), pp. 27–8.
5 *Ibid.*, p. 29.
6 Sarah Benton, citing R. Beange, J. Curtice and R. Spencer, 'Britain's Parliamentary Battleground', *New Statesman and Society*, 16 August, 1991, p. 8.
7 P. Dunleavy, *New Statesman and Society*, 16 September 1988, pp. 13–15.

Appendix 1: Key Dates, 1945–1992

1945	July	Liberals win 12 seats in general election. Clement Davies elected Chairman of Parliamentary Party.
1950	February	Nine Liberal MPs returned in general election. 319 of 475 Liberal candidates lose their deposits.
1951	May	Six Liberals returned at general election. Churchill offers Clement Davies the Ministry of Education. He declines the offer.
1956		Davies resigns leadership. Jo Grimond elected Chairman of the Liberal MPs.
1958	March	Mark Bonham-Carter wins Torrington by-election, first Liberal by-election victory since 1929.
1959	October	Liberals win six seats at general election.
1962	March	Eric Lubbock wins Orpington by-election.
1964	October	Liberals win nine seats in general election.
1965	March	David Steel wins Roxburgh, Selkirk and Peebles by-election.
1966	March	Liberals win 12 seats in general election.
1967	January	Grimond resigns. Jeremy Thorpe elected Chairman of Liberal MPs.

1970	June	Liberals win six seats in general election.
1972-3		Dramatic series of Liberal by-election victories in Rochdale, Sutton, Ely, Ripon and Berwick.
1974	February	Liberals win 14 seats in general election; Heath approaches Thorpe with offer of a coalition but talks break down when Heath refuses to promise electoral reform.
	October	Librals win 13 seats in general election.
1976	May	Thorpe resigns after party pressure following the Norman Scott affair. 'Interregnum' leadership by Grimond and Steel until Steel elected leader of the Party.
1977	March	Liberals enter Lib-Lab Pact to sustain minority Callaghan Government.
1978	May	Liberals withdraw from Lib-Lab Pact.
1979	May	Liberals win 11 seats in general election.
1981	March	Formation of the Social Democratic Party.
	September	Liberals and SDP form Alliance.
1983	June	Alliance win 26 per cent of the vote in the general election but only 23 seats.
1986	September	Eastbourne conference passes non-nuclear amendment in opposition to leadership. Alliance slumps in polls.
1987	June	Alliance wins 22 seats in the general election with 23 per cent of the vote. David Steel immediately calls for a merger of the two parties; David Owen opposes merger and resigns as leader of the SDP.
1988	January	Liberal and SDP special conferences vote for merger of the two parties and

formation of the Social and Liberal Democrats.

	March	Launch of the new Social and Liberal Democratss. David Owen forms 'continuing SDP'.
	June	David Steel announces he will not stand in forthcoming leadership contest.
	July	Ashdown elected leader of Social and Liberal Democrats.
1989	February	Rival SLD and SDP candidates split the Alliance share of the vote at the Richmond (Yorks.) by-election allowing Conservative victory.
		Poll of SLD members agrees to adopt short title of Liberal Democrats.
	June	Liberal Democrats pushed into fourth place in the direct elections to the European Parliament following surge in Green Party support.
1990	May	Liberal Democrats manage to retain credible level of support in local elections. Continuing SDP faces impracticality of maintaining a nationwide presence.
	June	SDP decides to cease campaigning as a political party.
1990	October	Liberal Democrats secure victory at the Eastbourne by-election in the wake of widespread opposition to the Poll Tax.
	November	Replacement of Mrs Thatcher with John Major as Prime Minister and Conservative leader.
1991	March	Liberal Democrats win Ribble Valley by-election, effectively ending Conservative attempts to retain the Poll Tax.

	May	Extensive Liberal Democrat gains in local elections.
	October	Liberal Democrat Conference supports Ashdown in programme of extra spending on education, 'green' taxes on fuel and pro-federalism in Europe.
1992	February	Ashdown survives revelation of former affair and his handling of the crisis boosts poll ratings.
	April	Liberal Democrats secure 20 MPs in general election on 18.3 per cent share of the vote, but fail to secure the balance of power in outright Conservative victory.

Appendix 2: Third Party Performance (Liberals, 1945–1979, Alliance 1981–1987, Liberal Democrats 1992)

Election	Seats won	Share of total vote (%)	No. of candidates	Lost deposits
1945	12	9.0	306	76
1950	9	9.1	475	319
1951	6	2.5	109	66
1955	6	2.7	110	60
1959	6	5.9	216	55
1964	9	11.2	365	52
1966	12	8.5	311	104
1970	6	7.5	332	184
1974 (Feb)	14	19.3	517	23
1974 (Oct)	13	18.5	619	125
1979	11	13.8	577	303
1983	17	25.4	633	10
1987	22	22.6	633	25
1992	20	18.3	631	11

Suggestions for Further Reading

Ball, A.R. *British Political Parties: the Emergence of a Modern Party System*, Macmillan, London, 1987.

Bogdanor, V. *Liberal Party Politics*, Oxford University Press, Oxford, 1983.

Bradley, I. *Breaking the Mould? The Birth and Prospects of the Social Democratic Party*, Martin Robertson, London, 1981.

Butler, D. *The Electoral System in Britain, 1918–1951*, Basil Blackwell, Oxford, 1953.

Butler, D. *British General Elections since 1945*, Basil Blackwell, Oxford, 1989.

Butler, D. and Butler, G. *British Political Facts, 1900–1985*, Macmillan, London, 1986.

Callaghan, J. *The Far Left in English Politics*, Basil Blackwell, Oxford, 1987.

Cook, C. *A Short History of the Liberal Party, 1900–1988*, Macmillan, Oxford, 1989.

Heath, A., Jowell, R. and Curtice, J. *How Britain Votes*, Pergamon, Oxford, 1985.

Heath, A., Curtice, J., Evans, G., Jowell, R., Field, J. and Witherspoon, S. *Understanding Political Change*, Pergamon, Oxford, 1991.

Ingle, S. *The British Party System*, 2nd edn, Basil Blackwell, Oxford, 1989.

Jenkins, R. *A Life at the Centre*, Macmillan, London, 1991.

Owen, D. *Face the Future*, Oxford University Press, Oxford, 1981.

Penniman, H.R. (ed.), *Britain at the Polls, 1979: A Study of the General Election*, American Enterprise Institute, London and Washington, 1981.

Seldon, A. (ed.), *UK Political Parties since 1945*, Philip Allan, Hemel Hempstead, 1990.

Smyth, G. (ed.) *Can the Tories Lose? The Battle for the Marginals*, Lawrence and Wishart, London, 1991.

Steel, D. *Against Goliath: David Steel's Story*, Weidenfeld and Nicolson, London, 1989.

Taylor, S. *The National Front in English Politics*, Macmillan, London, 1982.

Williams, S. *Politics is for People*, Penguin, Harmondsworth, 1981.

Index

DUDLEY D/3
(174)